"'一带一路'与粤港澳大湾区特色教材"研究成果

实用交际汉语 3
Practical Communicative Chinese

王功平 编著

北京语言大学出版社
BEIJING LANGUAGE AND CULTURE
UNIVERSITY PRESS

© 2023 北京语言大学出版社，社图号 23217

图书在版编目（CIP）数据

实用交际汉语. 3 / 王功平编著. – 北京：北京语言大学出版社，2023.12
ISBN 978-7-5619-6436-1

Ⅰ. ①实… Ⅱ. ①王… Ⅲ. ①汉语－口语－对外汉语教学－教材 Ⅳ. ①H195.4

中国国家版本馆 CIP 数据核字 (2023) 第 232140 号

实用交际汉语 3
SHIYONG JIAOJI HANYU 3

版式设计：	邱 彬　黄 莉	
排版制作：	北京青侣文化创意设计有限公司	
图片提供：	王功平　壹图网	
责任印制：	周　燚	

出版发行： 北京语言大学出版社
社　　址： 北京市海淀区学院路 15 号，100083
网　　址： www.blcup.com
电子信箱： service@blcup.com
电　　话： 编辑部　　8610-82303647/3592/3395
　　　　　　　国内发行　8610-82303650/3591/3648
　　　　　　　海外发行　8610-82303365/3080/3668
　　　　　　　北语书店　8610-82303653
　　　　　　　网购咨询　8610-82303908
印　　刷： 天津嘉恒印务有限公司

版　　次： 2023 年 12 月第 1 版　　　**印　　次：** 2023 年 12 月第 1 次印刷
开　　本： 787 毫米 × 1092 毫米　1/16　**印　　张：** 18.25
字　　数： 207 千字
定　　价： 72.00 元

PRINTED IN CHINA

凡有印装质量问题，本社负责调换。售后QQ号1367565611，电话010-82303590

前　言

《实用交际汉语》是"'一带一路'与粤港澳大湾区特色教材"的研究成果。本套教材以培养汉语学习者的汉语交际能力为核心，侧重面向"一带一路"国家的初级汉语学习者。教材既适用于正式在校的学习者，也适用于补习班或者个人辅导班的学习者；既适用于初学汉语的中小学生，也适用于广大成人初级汉语学习者。

全套教材共4册。考虑到有的海外国家采用一年三学期制，每学期除了节日和复习考试外，实际上课12周，同时考虑到不同学校开设汉语课的周学时有差异，我们按照平均每周2次课、每次2个课时的教学时间安排内容。每册共计24课，包括6大项24小项的交际功能和两个综合实践训练。这些交际功能包括"见面问候""请求帮助""购物讲价""体育健身""看病就医""旅游观光"等，可以满足学习者日常生活、学习和出行的常用交际需求。

本套教材在编写过程中主要遵循如下思路：

采用意验大纲

教材的编写既突破早期以字词为纲的理念，也突破后来以结构（语法）为纲的理念，同时还突破以功能（交际功能）为纲的理念，主要采用意验大纲，同时兼顾字词和语法的难度等级。这里的"意验"主要指学习者跟随本教材学习汉语的过程，也是运用汉语发展交际意识、体验交际功能和文化的过程。比如，学习者通过学习第一册的第一至三课及第十课，就可以掌握在不同场合中与不同年龄、身份的人见面时打招呼的方式；同时，在学习过程中体验打招呼的不同方式之间的汉语用语差异。其中，第一课安排的交际功能为生人之间的见面及问候，第二、三课安排的交际功能为熟人之间的见面及问候，而第十课安排的交际功能则为在正式场合下礼貌地询问他人姓名的方式。这样的次序又兼顾了字词、语法、功能和文化的难易程度。

紧紧围绕一个目标

教材坚持以培养学习者的汉语交际能力为核心，让学习者多层次、全方位地了解中国，包括中国的历史和现状，中国的社会、经济、科技、文化等各个领域的发展情况。

坚持两翼并举

教材坚持听力和口语两大技能齐头并进，以听带说，以说促听。

努力做到三驾齐驱

教材努力做到语言、文化和科技三驾齐驱，以掌握语言（汉语）为基础，以了解文化为目标，以科学的载体为推进器，适应移动学习（M-Learning）、即时学习（Just-in-Time Learning）、掌上学习（P-Learning）的需求。

切实实现五管齐下

（1）交际性。每课话题的选取、语法点的讲解、文化点的介绍、课后练习的设计都紧紧围绕"提高学习者的汉语交际能力"这一核心目标。（2）真实性。教材中课文的语料均来源于真实的生活，服务于真实的交际场景。（3）适用性。教材适用于不同母语或第一语言背景及不同汉语水平的学习者。（4）科学性。教材的所有生词、语法点和交际话题的选取、排序，均参考了学界的权威大纲，比如《汉语水平等级标准与语法等级大纲》《高等学校外国留学生汉语言专业教学大纲》（附件二）、《国际汉语教学通用课程大纲》及《国际中文教育中文水平等级标准》等。（5）趣味性。主要包括内容的趣味性和形式的趣味性，不同的课文相互衔接成完整的故事，学习者可以在"交"（交际）中学，也可以在学中"交"（交际）。

协调好五大关系

（1）中与外的关系。教材内容不全是关于中国的，也有关于世界其他国家的，比如世界杯、母亲节等，以增强对学习者的亲和力。（2）古与今的关系。教材内容既介绍了中国古代的成就，也讲述了中国当今社会的方方面面。（3）语与文的关系。语言和文化紧密相连，水乳交融，相互促进。教材每课都配备一个与本课内容相关的"文化小常识"，方便学习者在学习汉语的同时，更深入地了解中国文化。（4）学与用的关系。教材注重使学习者在学中用，以用促学；让学习者感到学有所用，用有所得，学起来轻松，用起来顺手。（5）俗与雅的关系。教材的内容既包括通俗的日常交际话题和用语，也包括文雅的正式交际话题和用语。

教材的体例安排如下：每课均在标题下给出该课的学习重点提示，主要内容则包括看图讨论、课文对话、生词注释、主要语言点讲解、文化小常识介绍、练习与实践六大部分。其中，看图讨论部分图文并茂，紧扣主题，抛砖引玉。课文内容真实、生动，人物对话既独立成篇，又注意有机统一、前后连贯。各课之间相互联系，环环相扣，引人入胜。对话交际项目的选取，既遵循学习者由易到难的学习规律，又符合社会发展趋势，紧扣时代脉搏。主要语言点讲解部分重点突出，句法、语义、语用结合，尤其突出交际功能的讲解。例句简单、实用，并附动画视频，视频中的文字不追求与课文内容一一对应，但求为学生提供身临其境的交际场景的体验。文化小常识介绍以点带面，重点突出，系统全面。练习与实践部分题型灵活，形式多样，内容丰富，既紧扣课文，又有拓展及延伸，与课文形成阶梯式爬坡，以满足不同水平学习者的需要。

本套教材的特色在于：（1）以先进的语言教学理论为指导，尤其注重吸收国际上先进的二语教学理念和教材编写理论。（2）有丰富的习得研究成果和教学经验的支撑，切实做到融汉语知识体系、二语习得规律和汉语教学经验于一炉。（3）交际话题具有真实性、实用性，教材所有话题均源于实践，并且加以条理化、系统化。（4）灵活运用新技术，打造多媒体资源支持的立体化教材。教材配以丰富的图片、录音、动画视频及汉字动态书写演示图等丰富的学习资源，以保证课堂教学真实化、生活化，学生课后复习自主化、随时化。

我们还将为教材的使用者（包括汉语学习者和国际汉语教师）提供灵活多样的教材使用服务，包括提供配套的汉字、语法学习资源，为汉语教师提供适用的教学课件，并适时组织相关教师进行教材使用培训和教学指导等。

为使本套教材能更好地服务广大汉语学习者和国际汉语教师，恳请大家在使用过程中提出宝贵的意见和建议。各位朋友递送意见或建议的联系方式为：1922418845@qq.com（电子邮箱）、pingw0159（微信号）。

暨南大学　王功平
2023 年 3 月

目 录

交际项目一　介绍人

第一课　我来自中国北京 ……………………………………… 2
　　　　交际功能 1：自我介绍

第二课　这是我的同学马文 …………………………………… 13
　　　　交际功能 2：介绍他人

第三课　这位是汉语系主任王文教授 ………………………… 23
　　　　交际功能 3：介绍嘉宾

交际项目二　介绍事物

第四课　您能介绍一下儿暨南大学吗 ………………………… 34
　　　　交际功能 4：介绍大学

第五课　中医有什么特点呢 …………………………………… 45
　　　　交际功能 5：介绍中医

第六课　喝茶有什么好处呢 …………………………………… 57
　　　　交际功能 6：讨论喝茶的好处

交际项目三　说明

第七课　我想参加 HSK 培训班 ………………………………… 68
　　　　交际功能 7：咨询培训班

i

第八课　我可以借更长时间吗 ················· 78
　　　　交际功能 8：在图书馆借书
第九课　你为什么想来我们公司工作呢 ··········· 87
　　　　交际功能 9：工作面试

综合实践一

第十课　我想申请中国政府奖学金 ··············· 100
　　　　交际功能 10：咨询奖学金申请的注意事项
第十一课　我想办理留学签证 ··················· 111
　　　　交际功能 11：办理留学签证
第十二课　我想咨询一下儿广交会的事 ··········· 121
　　　　交际功能 12：咨询广交会

交际项目四　谈论天气

第十三课　今天的天气怎么样 ··················· 134
　　　　交际功能 13：谈论天气
第十四课　今天的气温有多高 ··················· 145
　　　　交际功能 14：谈论气温
第十五课　中国的气候怎么样 ··················· 157
　　　　交际功能 15：谈论气候

交际项目五　谈论旅游

第十六课　我们出去郊游吧 ····················· 168
　　　　交际功能 16：讨论郊游安排
第十七课　你觉得跟团游怎么样 ················· 180
　　　　交际功能 17：谈论跟团游

第十八课　我打算参加出境游 ·············· 191

　　　　　交际功能 18：谈论出境游

交际项目六　　出行交通

第十九课　高速公路会不会堵车呢 ·············· 202

　　　　　交际功能 19：谈论高速公路

第二十课　高铁既快速又准时 ·············· 212

　　　　　交际功能 20：谈论高铁出行

第二十一课　我的行李超重了没有 ·············· 222

　　　　　交际功能 21：谈论乘机出行

综合实践二

第二十二课　您想订什么样的房间 ·············· 234

　　　　　交际功能 22：办理酒店入住手续

第二十三课　请问您要打车吗 ·············· 245

　　　　　交际功能 23：谈论乘坐出租车

第二十四课　我想改签一下儿机票，可以吗 ·············· 255

　　　　　交际功能 24：改签机票

生词表 ·············· 266

致谢 ·············· 280

交际项目一
介绍人

第一课 Lesson 1

Wǒ láizì Zhōngguó Běijīng
我来自中国北京

重点提示

- 交际功能：自我介绍。
- 主要生词：来自、高兴、开心、从事、电脑、工作、名片。
- 主要语言点：很高兴+动词短语，来自……，从事……。
- 文化小常识：个人名片

一 看图讨论 Look at the picture and discuss

1. 他们在做什么？ What are they doing?
2. 他们会说什么呢？ What might they say?

二 》 课 文 Text

听录音回答问题 Listen to the recording and answer the following questions.

1. 他们在做什么？ What are they doing?
2. 马文是哪里人？做什么工作？ Where is Ma Wen from? What does he do?
3. 李安平是哪里人？做什么工作？ Where is Li Anping from? What does she do?

Wǒ láizì Zhōngguó Běijīng
我来自 中国 北京 1-1

Lǐ Ānpíng: 李安平：	Nǐ hǎo, wǒ shì Lǐ Ānpíng. Hěn gāoxìng rènshi nǐ. 你好，我是李安平。很 高兴 认识你。
Mǎ Wén: 马 文：	Nǐ hǎo, wǒ shì Mǎ Wén. Rènshi nǐ, wǒ yě hěn kāixīn. 你好，我是马文。认识你，我也很开心。
Lǐ Ānpíng: 李安平：	Wǒ láizì Zhōngguó Běijīng, shì yì míng Hànyǔ jiàoshī. 我来自 中国 北京，是一名 汉语 教师。
Mǎ Wén: 马 文：	Wǒ láizì Tàiguó Màngǔ, cóngshì diànnǎo fāngmiàn de gōngzuò. 我来自泰国曼谷，从事 电脑 方面 的 工作。
Lǐ Ānpíng: 李安平：	Huānyíng nǐ! Zhè shì wǒ de míngpiàn. 欢迎 你！这是我的 名片。
Mǎ Wén: 马 文：	Xièxie! Zhè shì wǒ de. 谢谢！这是我的。

Lǐ Ānpíng:	Qǐng duō liánxì!
李安平：	请多联系！

Mǎ Wén:	Hǎo de, bǎochí liánxì!
马文：	好的，保持联系！

三 生词 New words 🔊 1-2

1. 来自	动词	láizì	come from
2. 高兴	形容词	gāoxìng	happy
3. 开心	形容词	kāixīn	glad
4. 名	量词	míng	*a measure word for people*
5. 汉语	专有名词	Hànyǔ	Chinese language
6. 教师	名词	jiàoshī	teacher
7. 曼谷	专有名词	Màngǔ	Bangkok
8. 从事	动词	cóngshì	be engaged in
9. 电脑	名词	diànnǎo	computer
10. 方面	名词	fāngmiàn	aspect
11. 工作	名词	gōngzuò	work, job
12. 名片	名词	míngpiàn	business card
13. 联系	动词	liánxì	contact

四 主要语言点 Main language points

1 很高兴认识你。

"很高兴＋动词短语"意思是说话人很高兴、很乐意做某事，是一句常用的客套用语，用于表示亲近、友好的关系。例如：

"很高兴 + verb phrase" means that the speaker is very happy to do something. It's a common polite expression used to express close and friendly relations. For example:

（1）很高兴认识你。
（2）很高兴参加这次比赛。
（3）很高兴和大家见面。

▷ 视频：1.1 很高兴……

2 我来自中国北京。

"来自……"是一句常用的介绍自己或他人籍贯、国籍等方面信息的用语。"来自"后面常接国家名或城市名等，意思是"从什么地方来"，相当于说"某人是哪里人"，多用于比较正式的场合。例如：

"来自……" is a commonly used expression to introduce one's own or others' native place, nationality, etc. "来自" is often followed by the name of a country or a city, meaning "from where", which is equivalent to "where someone is from". It is mostly used on formal occasions. For example:

(1) 我来自中国香港。
(2) 马文来自泰国。
(3) 李平来自马来西亚。
(4) 王老师来自中国广东。

视频：1.2 我来自中国北京。

3 我从事电脑方面的工作。

"从事……"是一句常用的介绍自己或他人工作、职业等方面信息的用语。"从事"后面多接表示工作、职业之类的名词或名词短语，常用于比较正式的场合。例如：

"从事……" is a commonly used expression to give an account of one's own or others' work and occupation. "从事" is often followed by a noun or noun phrase indicating work, occupation, etc. It is often used on formal occasions. For example:

(1) 我从事华文（Huáwén）教育（jiàoyù）工作。
(2) 马文从事会计（kuàijì）工作。
(3) 她从事护理（hùlǐ）工作。
(4) 我的哥哥从事商贸（shāngmào）工作。

视频：1.2 我来自中国北京。

五 〉〉 文化小常识 General knowledge of culture

个人名片

个人名片是第一次与人见面时，用来介绍自己姓名、学历、职称、职务、工作单位、联系地址和电话号码等基本信息的小卡片。中文名片要注意姓名、工作单位、联系地址等信息的书写顺序。姓名的顺序是姓在前、名在后，如"王云平"。单位和地址都是按从大到小的顺序排列，如"清华大学人文学院中国语言文学系""北京市海淀区双清路30号"。

Personal Business Card

A personal business card is a small card given to someone meeting for the first time to introduce one's name, education background, professional title, position, workplace, contact address, phone number and other basic information. Note the order of the information on a Chinese business card, such as one's name, workplace and contact address. A Chinese person's family name comes before his/her given name, such as "王云平". His/her workplace and contact address are arranged in descending order, such as "清华大学人文学院中国语言文学系", "北京市海淀区双清路30号".

实用交际汉语 3
Practical Communicative Chinese

六 练习与实践 Exercises and practice

1 听录音，选择你听到的音，然后朗读下面的拼音。 🔊 1–3

Listen to the recording and choose the pronunciation you hear, then read the following Pinyin aloud.

(1) rènshi　rénshì
　　认识　— 人事

(2) míngtiān　míngpiàn
　　明天　— 名片

(3) kāixīn　gāoxìng
　　开心　— 高兴

(4) láiqù　láizì
　　来去　— 来自

(5) cóngshì　zǒngshì
　　从事　— 总是

(6) jiàoshī　jiàoshì
　　教师　— 教室

(7) liànxí　liánxì
　　练习　— 联系

(8) diànnǎo　tiánhǎo
　　电脑　— 填好

2 朗读下面的句子，注意停顿和重音。

Read the following sentences aloud, paying attention to the pause and stress.

(1) 很高兴认识你。

(2) 我来自中国北京，是一名汉语教师。

(3) 欢迎你！这是我的名片。

(4) 请多联系！

(5) 保持联系！

3 选词填空。

Choose the right words to fill in the blanks.

| 认识　高兴　来自　联系　开心　从事　教学　名片 |

A：你＿＿＿＿我们的汉语老师吗？

B：认识，他＿＿＿＿中国广州。这是他给我的＿＿＿＿。

A：太好了，我正好想＿＿＿＿他，真是太＿＿＿＿了。

B：我也很＿＿＿＿能帮到你。

A：我们的汉语老师怎么样？

B：他＿＿＿＿汉语＿＿＿＿工作已经很多年了，水平很高。

4 连词成句。

Arrange the words to make sentences.

（1）我　很　认识　你　开心　也

_____。

（2）泰国　工作　我　来自　教学　曼谷　从事　汉语

_____。

（3）中国　医生　我　来自　是　一名　香港

_____。

（4）来自　从事　她　方面　电脑　北京　的　工作

_____。

（5）高兴　这　参加　很　次　会议

_____。

实用交际汉语 3
Practical Communicative Chinese

5 替换练习。
Substitution drills.

（1）我来自<u>清华大学</u>，从事<u>计算机研究</u>。

香港中文大学	汉语教学工作
中央电视台	主持（zhǔchí）工作
第一医院	医务（yīwù）工作

（2）他来自<u>泰国曼谷</u>，从事<u>电脑方面的工作</u>。

新加坡	华文教学工作
马来西亚	商务工作
越南（Yuènán）	翻译（fānyì）工作

（3）很高兴<u>认识您</u>。

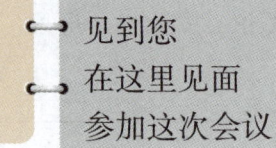

见到您
在这里见面
参加这次会议

6 完成下面的对话，然后和同学一起表演对话的内容。
Complete the following dialogues, then act them out with your classmates.

（1）男：你好！很高兴_____。

女：你好！_____我也很_____。

男：我_____法国，_____翻译工作。

女：我_____美国，_____汉语教学工作。

男：请多_____！

女：好的，保持_____！

（2）A：今天很_____听马老师的汉语课。

B：上马老师的汉语课，我们都很_____。

A：马老师_____汉语_____工作有多长时间了呢？

B：马老师_____汉语_____工作有二十多年了。

A：你经常和马老师_____吗？

B：是的，我们经常_____。

7 看视频，先回答问题，然后和同学一起表演视频的内容。
Watch the video and answer the questions. Then act out the video with your classmates.

（1）男的来自什么地方？从事什么工作？

（2）女的来自什么地方？从事什么工作？

▶ 视频：1.2 我来自中国北京。

8 设想自己认识了一位新朋友，用下面的词语介绍一下儿自己。
Suppose you meet a new friend. Introduce yourself with the following words.

认识   高兴   来自   从事   工作   联系

9 汉字练习：看汉字笔画笔顺动态图，并跟着书写。
Practice Chinese characters: Look at the animated illustrations of the strokes and the order of strokes of the following characters, and then write them down.

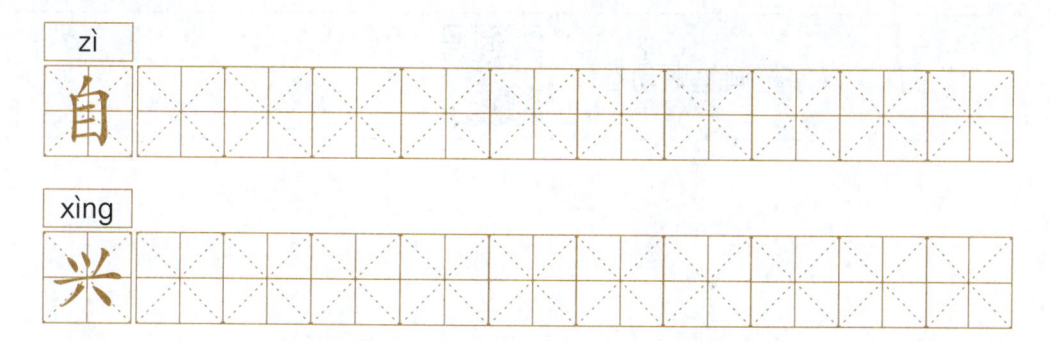

zì
自

xìng
兴

实用交际汉语 3

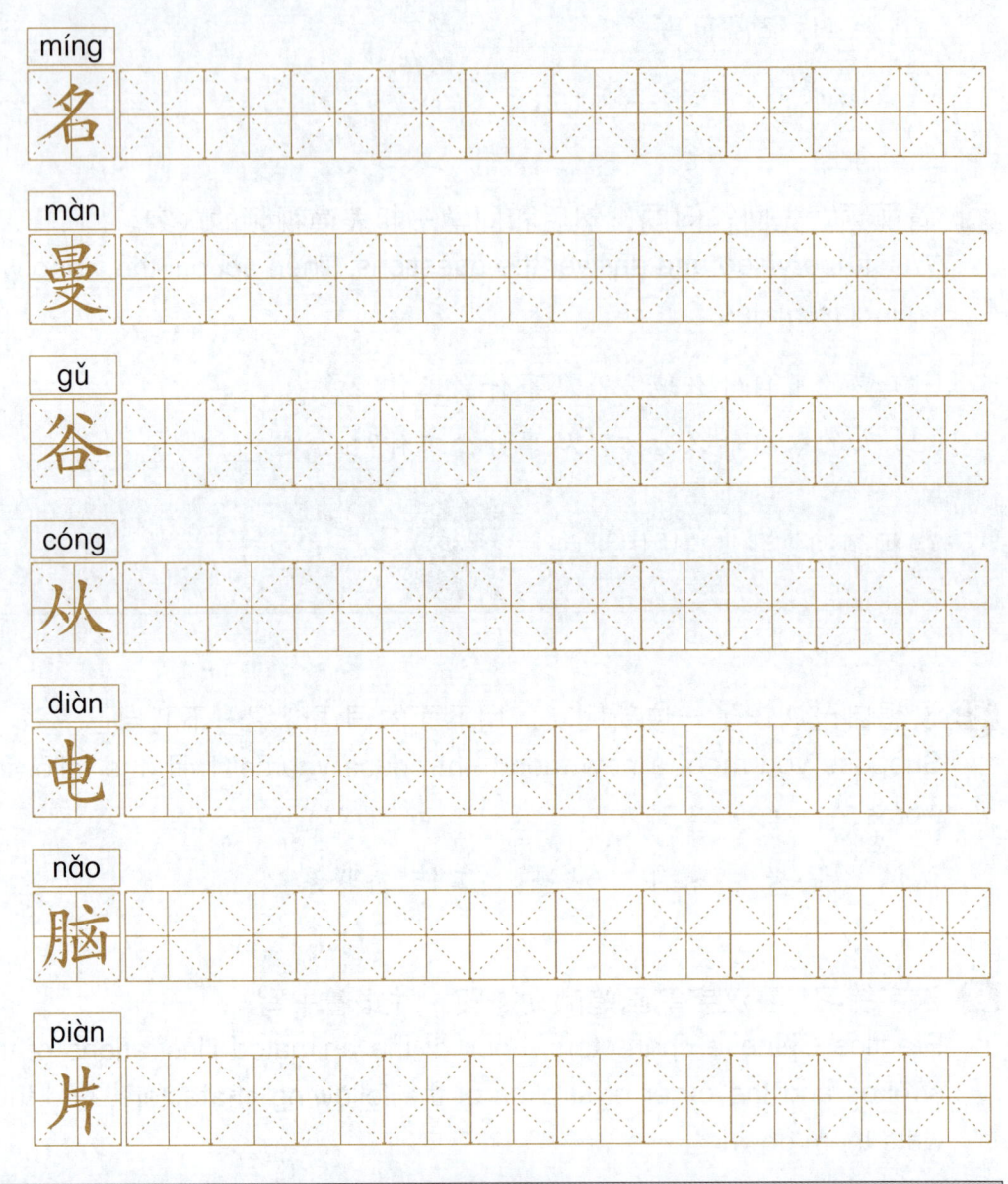

míng
名

màn
曼

gǔ
谷

cóng
从

diàn
电

nǎo
脑

piàn
片

第一课　汉字笔画笔顺动态图

第二课 Lesson 2

Zhè shì wǒ de tóngxué Mǎ Wén
这是我的同学马文

重点提示

- 交际功能：介绍他人。
- 主要生词：朋友、商贸、荣幸、以后。
- 主要语言点：语气词"啊"，同位语。
- 文化小常识：介绍他人的顺序。

一 看图讨论 Look at the picture and discuss

1. 他们在做什么？ What are they doing?
2. 他们会说什么呢？ What might they say?

二 课文 Text

听录音回答问题 Listen to the recording and answer the following questions.

1. 李安平在做什么？ What is Li Anping doing?
2. 安妮是哪里人？做什么工作？ Where is Anne from? What does she do?

Zhè shì wǒ de tóngxué Mǎ Wén
这是我的同学马文 2-1

Lǐ Ānpíng: Wǒ gěi nǐmen jièshào yíxiàr.
李安平：我给你们介绍一下儿。

Mǎ Wén、Ānnī: Hǎo a!
马文、安妮：好啊！

Lǐ Ānpíng: Zhè shì wǒ de tóngxué Mǎ Wén, láizì Tàiguó Màngǔ, cóngshì
李安平：这是我的同学马文，来自泰国曼谷，从事

diànnǎo fāngmiàn de gōngzuò.
电脑方面的工作。

Ānnī: Nǐ hǎo! Hěn gāoxìng rènshi nǐ.
安妮：你好！很高兴认识你。

Lǐ Ānpíng: Zhè shì wǒ de péngyou Ānnī, láizì Mǎláixīyà Jílóngpō,
李安平：这是我的朋友安妮，来自马来西亚吉隆坡，

cóngshì shāngmào gōngzuò.
从事商贸工作。

Mǎ Wén: Ānnī, nǐ hǎo! Hěn róngxìng jiàndào nǐ.
马 文：安妮，你好！很 荣幸 见到 你。

Lǐ Ānpíng: Wǒmen yǐhòu duō liánxì!
李安平：我们 以后 多 联系！

Mǎ Wén、Ānnī: Hǎo de, xièxie nǐ de jièshào.
马 文、安妮：好 的，谢谢 你 的 介绍。

三 》 生 词 New words 2-2

1. 安妮	专有名词	Ānnī	Anne, name of a person
2. 朋友	名词	péngyou	friend
3. 马来西亚	专有名词	Mǎláixīyà	Malaysia
4. 吉隆坡	专有名词	Jílóngpō	Kuala Lumpur
5. 商贸	名词	shāngmào	commerce and trade
6. 荣幸	形容词	róngxìng	honoured (to do sth.)
7. 以后	名词	yǐhòu	later time

四 主要语言点 Main language points

1 好啊！

这句中的"啊"是一个语气助词，用在陈述句末尾，使句子带上一层感情色彩，有加强肯定语气的作用。例如：

The modal particle "啊" in this sentence is used at the end of the declarative sentence, which adds an emotional touch to the sentence to reinforce the positive mood. For example:

（1）A：我给你介绍一下儿。
　　　B：好啊！
（2）A：下课后我们去外面吃饭吧。
　　　B：行啊！
（3）A：这个星期天我们去旅游，怎么样？
　　　B：好啊！
（4）A：我们请老师给我们讲解（jiǎngjiě）一下儿吧。
　　　B：可以啊！

▶ 视频：2.1 我给你们介绍一下儿。

注意："啊"的发音常受到前字读音的影响而发生不同的音变，书面上有时按音变写成不同的字。例如：

Note: The pronunciation of "啊" often varies with the finals of the syllables before it, and in written Chinese, the variants are sometimes represented by different characters. For example:

前字末尾音素	加"啊"	读作	写作
i、ü、a、o、e、ê	+a	→ ya [iA]	呀
u	+a	→ wa [uA]	哇
n	+a	→ na [nA]	哪
ng	+a	→ nga [ŋA]	啊
-i [ʅ], er	+a	→ ra [ʐA]	啊
-i [ɿ]	+a	→ [zA]	啊

2 这是我的同学马文。

这个句子中的"我的同学"和"马文"指的是同一个人，并且都做句子的宾语，因此叫作同位语。同位语，指在同一个句子中指代同一个人或事物，充当相同句子成分的两个并列的名词或名词短语。例如：

Both "我的同学" and "马文" in this sentence refer to the same person and both serve as the object of the sentence, so they are called appositives. An appositive refers to two parallel nouns or noun phrases indicating the same person or thing and act as the same component in the same sentence. For example:

（1）这是我的汉语老师王文平教授（jiàoshòu）。
（2）这是我的姐姐玛丽。
（3）那是我们的学校中山大学。
（4）这是我们最喜欢的电视剧《西游记》。

▶ 视频：2.1 我给你们介绍一下儿。

五 文化小常识 General knowledge of culture

介绍他人的顺序

在中国，当我们介绍他人时，要注意介绍的先后顺序。在年龄方面，应先介绍年长的，后介绍年轻的；在性别方面，应先介绍女士，后介绍男士；在职务级别方面，应先介绍级别比较高的，后介绍级别比较低的。

The Order of Introducing Others

In China, we should note the order of introduction when we introduce others. In terms of age, the senior should be introduced before young people; in terms of gender, women should be introduced before men; in terms of official rank, high-ranking officials should be introduced before low-ranking ones.

六 练习与实践 Exercises and practice

1 听录音，选择你听到的音，然后朗读下面的拼音。 2-3
Listen to the recording and choose the pronunciation you hear, then read the following Pinyin aloud.

（1）同学 — 冬 雪　　　　（2）朋友 — 笨 牛
　　 tóngxué dōng xuě　　　　　　péngyou bèn niú

　　　　jǐ kǒu　　yǐhòu　　　　　　　　róngxìng　cóngxīn
（3）几口 — 以后　　　　　（4）荣幸 — 从新

　　　　dàjiā　　Dàojiào　　　　　　　sòngdào　shāngmào
（5）大家 — 道教　　　　　（6）送到 — 商贸

2 朗读下面的句子，注意停顿和重音。
Read the following sentences aloud, paying attention to the pause and stress.

（1）我给你们介绍一下儿。
（2）这是我的朋友安妮。
（3）安妮从事商贸工作。
（4）很荣幸见到你！
（5）我们以后多联系！

3 连词成句。
Arrange the words to make sentences.

（1）是　这　我　的　马文　同学

　　　_____。

（2）给　一下儿　你们　介绍　我

　　　_____。

（3）到　你　很　荣幸　见

　　　_____。

（4）我的　这　老师　是　王文平　汉语　教授

　　　_____。

❹ 替换练习。
Substitution drills.

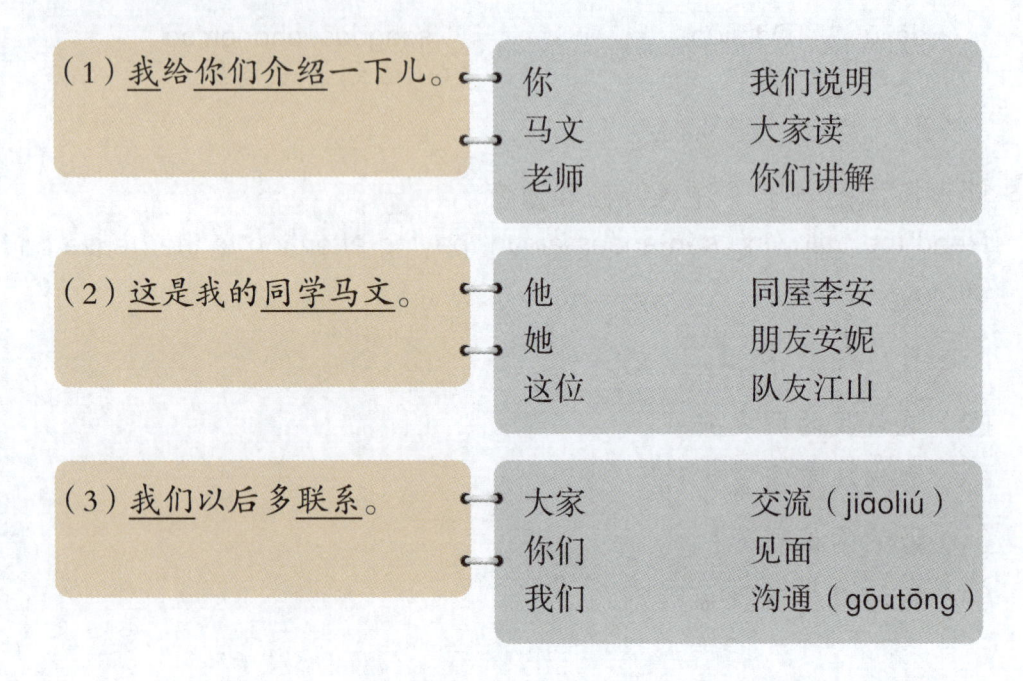

(1) 我给你们介绍一下儿。
   你　　　我们说明
   马文　　大家读
   老师　　你们讲解

(2) 这是我的同学马文。
   他　　　同屋李安
   她　　　朋友安妮
   这位　　队友江山

(3) 我们以后多联系。
   大家　　交流（jiāoliú）
   你们　　见面
   我们　　沟通（gōutōng）

❺ 完成下面的对话，然后和同学一起表演对话的内容。
Complete the following dialogues, then act them out with your classmates.

(1) 老　师：我_____大家介绍一下儿。

   同学们：好_____！

   老　师：_____我们班新来的同学安妮。

   安　妮：_____认识大家。

   老　师：希望大家以后_____交流。

(2) A：我_____你们介绍一下儿。

   B：好的，谢谢！

   A：_____是我们的队长李平。

   B：_____认识你。

   C：认识你我也_____。

第二课 这是我的同学马文

6 看视频，先回答问题，然后和同学一起表演视频的内容。
Watch the video and answer the questions. Then act out the video with your classmates.

（1）李安平介绍了谁？

（2）他是李安平的什么人？

（3）他是哪里人？做什么工作？

▶ 视频：2.1 我给你们介绍一下儿。

7 设想自己邀请同学到家里做客，用下面的词语给同学和家里人做一下儿介绍。

Suppose you invite your classmates over. Introduce your classmates and family members with the following words.

介绍　给　认识　这位　以后　见到　联系

8 汉字练习：看汉字笔画笔顺动态图，并跟着书写。
Practice Chinese characters: Look at the animated illustrations of the strokes and the order of strokes of the following characters, and then write them down.

| nī |
| 妮 |

| péng |
| 朋 |

| mǎ |
| 马 |

yà
亚

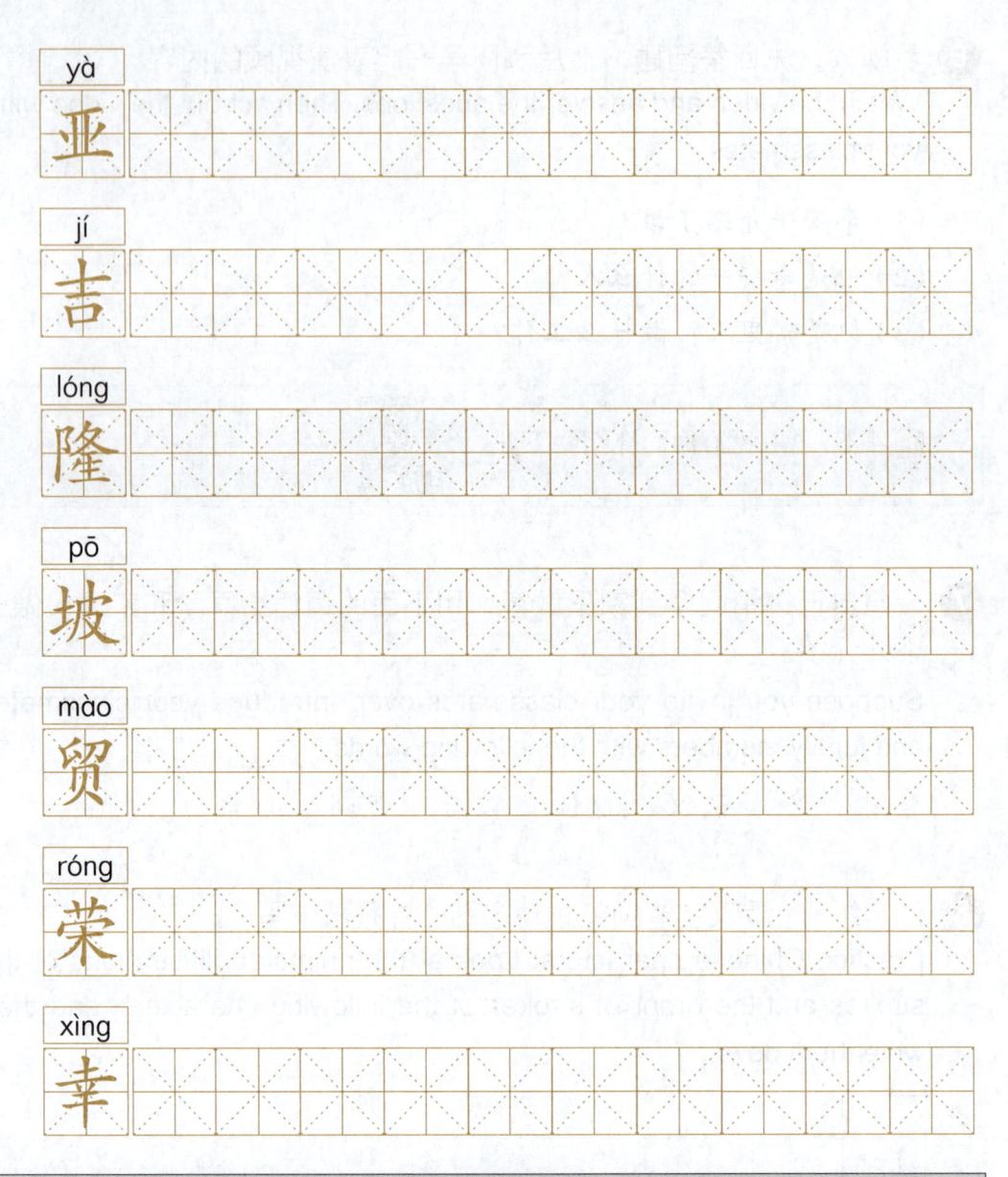

jí
吉

lóng
隆

pō
坡

mào
贸

róng
荣

xìng
幸

第二课　汉字笔画笔顺动态图

第三课 Lesson 3

Zhè wèi shì Hànyǔ Xì zhǔrèn
这位是汉语系主任
Wáng Wén jiàoshòu
王 文 教授

重点提示

- 交际功能：介绍嘉宾。
- 主要生词：主任、教授、允许、嘉宾、大会、公司、经理、邀请。
- 主要语言点：请允许我……，这位是……。
- 文化小常识：介绍他人身份的方式。

一 看图讨论 Look at the picture and discuss

1. 他们在做什么？ What are they doing?
2. 主持人会怎么介绍嘉宾呢？ How will the host introduce the guests?

二 课文 Text

听录音回答问题 Listen to the recording and answer the following questions.

1. 主持人在做什么？ What is the host doing?
2. 主持人会说什么？ What might the host say?

这位是汉语系主任王文教授
Zhè wèi shì Hànyǔ Xì zhǔrèn Wáng Wén jiàoshòu

3-1

zhúchírén: Qǐng yǔnxǔ wǒ jièshào yíxiàr wǒmen de jiābīn.
主持人： 请允许我介绍一下儿我们的嘉宾。

dàjiā: Xièxie!
大家： 谢谢！

zhúchírén: Zhè wèi shì wǒmen de lǎo péngyou Mǎ Lì xiānsheng.
主持人： 这位是我们的老朋友马力先生。

Mǎ Lì: Xièxie! Hěn gāoxìng hé dàjiā jiànmiàn!
马力： 谢谢！很高兴和大家见面！

zhúchírén: Zhè wèi shì Hànyǔ Xì zhǔrèn Wáng Wén jiàoshòu.
主持人： 这位是汉语系主任王文教授。

Wáng Wén: Xièxie! Hěn gāoxìng cānjiā běn cì dàhuì.
王文： 谢谢！很高兴参加本次大会。

zhúchírén: Zhè wèi shì Chángxìn Gōngsī jīnglǐ Jiāng Shān nǚshì.
主持人： 这位是长信公司经理江山女士。

Jiāng Shān: Xièxie! Gǎnxiè dàjiā de yāoqǐng!
江　山：谢谢！感谢大家的邀请！

三　生词　New words　3-2

1. 主任	名词	zhǔrèn	director
2. 王文	专有名词	Wáng Wén	Wang Wen, name of a person
3. 教授	名词	jiàoshòu	professor
4. 主持人	名词	zhǔchírén	host/hostess
5. 允许	动词	yǔnxǔ	allow
6. 嘉宾	名词	jiābīn	honoured guest
7. 老	形容词	lǎo	of long standing, old
8. 马力	专有名词	Mǎ Lì	Ma Li, name of a person
9. 先生	名词	xiānsheng	Mr., sir
10. 本	代词	běn	this
11. 大会	名词	dàhuì	conference
12. 长信公司	专有名词	Chángxìn Gōngsī	Changxin Company
公司	名词	gōngsī	company
13. 经理	名词	jīnglǐ	manager
14. 女士	名词	nǚshì	Ms., madam
15. 感谢	动词	gǎnxiè	thank
16. 邀请	动词	yāoqǐng	invite

四 主要语言点 Main language points

1 请允许我介绍一下儿我们的嘉宾。

"请允许＋我＋动词……"表示很客气、很礼貌地请求别人同意自己做某事，多用于会议、典礼等正式场合。例如：

"请允许＋我＋verb……" is used to politely ask for permission to do something. It is mostly used in meetings, ceremonies, and other formal occasions. For example:

（1）请允许我做一下儿自我（zìwǒ）介绍。
（2）请允许我给大家介绍一下儿这里的客人。
（3）请允许我欢迎新同学的到来（dàolái）。

▶ 视频：3.1 请允许我……

2 这位是汉语系主任王文教授。

"这位是……"是在大型会议、典礼等正式场合介绍嘉宾的常用句型，含有尊重的意味。例如：

"这位是……" is a sentence pattern often used to introduce an honoured guest on formal occasions, such as conferences and ceremonies. It is used to show respect. For example:

（1）这位是我们的校长李安国教授。
（2）这位是足球队主力马文同学。
（3）这位是长信公司经理江山女士。

▶ 视频：3.2 这位是……

五 › 文化小常识 General knowledge of culture

介绍他人身份的方式

在正式场合中用汉语介绍他人身份时要特别注意:(1)介绍职务时,要先说明工作单位,接着说明职务,最后说出他人的全名,并且要在全名的后面加上"先生""教授"等称谓;(2)如果一个人有多个职务,要按照这些职务的大小或者重要程度等主次顺序进行介绍。

Ways to Introduce Someone's Identity

On formal occasions, special attention should be paid when introducing someone's identity in Chinese: (1) Workplace is introduced before the position, and then the person's full name, with titles such as "Mr.", "Professor" added after his/her full name; (2) For a person with many positions, the positions are introduced in order of priority, such as the level or importance.

六 › 练习与实践 Exercises and practice

1 听录音,选择你听到的音,然后朗读下面的拼音。 3-3
Listen to the recording and choose the pronunciation you hear, then read the following Pinyin aloud.

(1) yǔnxǔ — rénshǒu
　　允许 — 人手

(2) jiǎ pǐn — jiābīn
　　假品 — 嘉宾

（3）叫醒 — 邀请　　　　（4）教授 — 小舟
　　jiàoxǐng yāoqǐng　　　　　jiàoshòu xiǎo zhōu

（5）先生 — 前身　　　　（6）巨人 — 主任
　　xiānsheng qiánshēn　　　　jùrén zhǔrèn

（7）公司 — 空子　　　　（8）经理 — 尽力
　　gōngsī kòngzi　　　　　　jīnglǐ jìnlì

2 朗读下面的句子，注意停顿和重音。
Read the following sentences aloud, paying attention to the pause and stress.

（1）请允许我介绍一下儿我们的嘉宾。

（2）这位是我们的老朋友马力先生。

（3）很高兴和大家见面！

（4）这位是汉语系主任王文教授。

（5）很高兴参加本次大会。

（6）感谢大家的邀请！

3 连线组成短语，并读一读。
Match the words to make phrases and read them.

请　　　　　　　　大会
介绍　　　　　　　系
汉语　　　　　　　允许
参加　　　　　　　经理
系　　　　　　　　一下儿
公司　　　　　　　主任

4 连词成句。
Arrange the words to make sentences.

(1) 我　允许　一下儿　嘉宾　介绍　请　我们的

_____。

(2) 我们的　位　马力　这　是　老朋友　先生

_____。

(3) 大会　很　参加　高兴　本　次

_____。

(4) 汉语系　这　王文　是　主任　位　教授

_____。

(5) 大家　邀请　的　感谢

_____！

5 替换练习。
Substitution drills.

(1) 请允许我<u>介绍一下儿</u>
　　<u>我们的嘉宾</u>。

　　介绍一下儿我自己
　　介绍一下儿我们的学校
　　说明一下儿这种手机的用法

(2) 这位是<u>汉语系主任</u> <u>王文教授</u>。

　　本校校长　　　　李立民教授
　　文化中心主任　　王明博士
　　长信公司经理　　江山女士

6 完成下面的对话，然后和同学一起表演对话的内容。
Complete the following dialogue, then act it out with your classmates.

A：请_____我介绍一下儿在座的嘉宾！_____是汉语系_____王平_____。

B：大家好！感谢大家的_____！

A：_____是长信公司_____江山_____。

C：很_____ _____本次大会。

7 看视频，先回答问题，然后和同学一起表演视频的内容。
Watch the video and answer the questions. Then act out the video with your classmates.

（1）主持人介绍了几位嘉宾？

（2）这几位嘉宾是什么身份（shēnfèn）？

▶ 视频：3.3 请允许我介绍一下儿我们的嘉宾。

8 设想自己将要主持一次学校活动，用下面的词语介绍一下儿到场的嘉宾。
Suppose you are going to host a school event. Introduce the guests with the following words.

允许　介绍　嘉宾　这位　主任　经理　校长

30

9 汉字练习：看汉字笔画笔顺动态图，并跟着书写。
Practice Chinese characters: Look at the animated illustrations of the strokes and the order of strokes of the following characters, and then write them down.

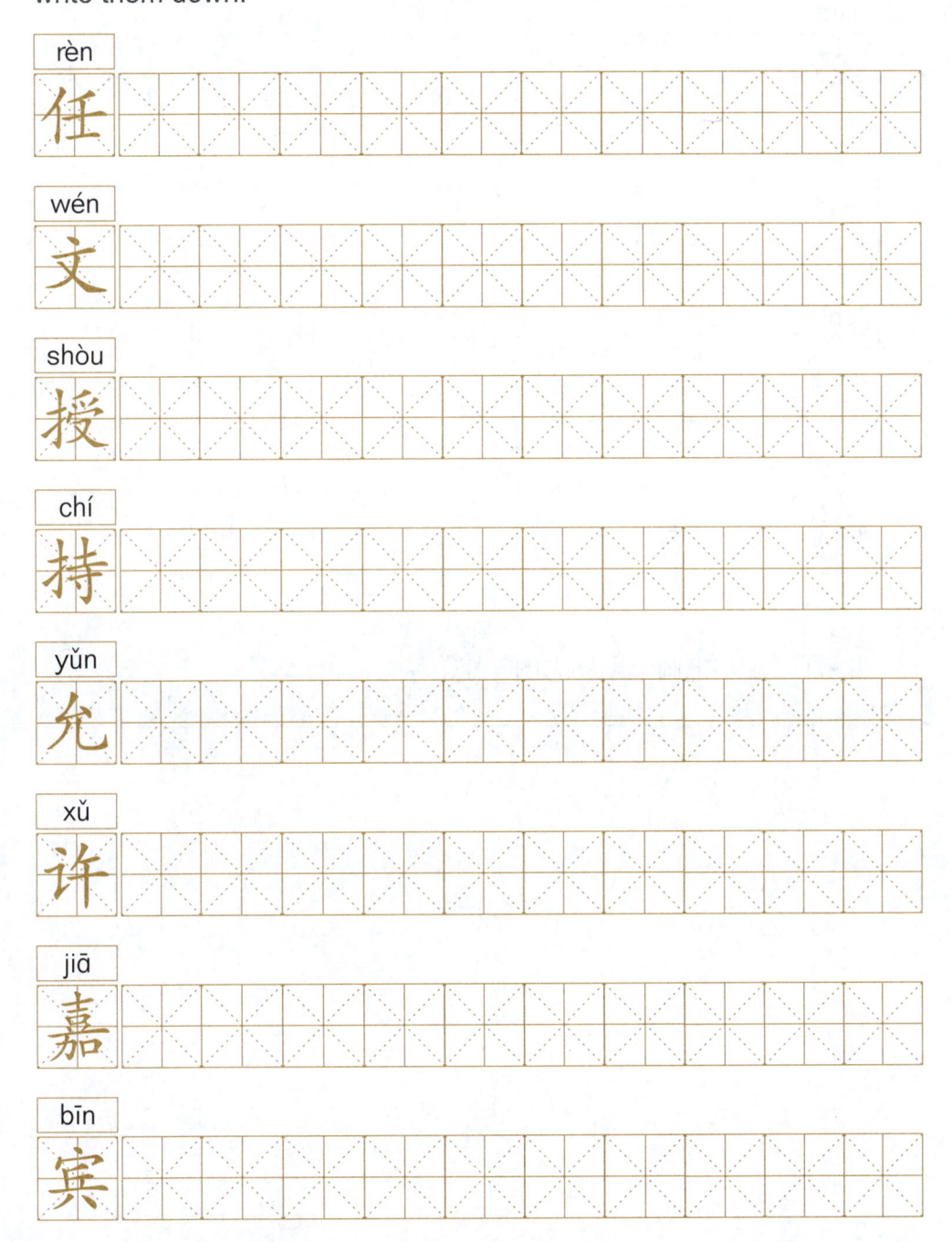

rèn
任

wén
文

shòu
授

chí
持

yǔn
允

xǔ
许

jiā
嘉

bīn
宾

sī
司

jīng
经

lǐ
理

shì
士

yāo
邀

第三课　汉字笔画笔顺动态图

交际项目二
介绍事物

第四课 Lesson 4

Nín néng jièshào yíxiàr Jìnán Dàxué ma
您能介绍一下儿暨南大学吗

重点提示

- **交际功能**：介绍大学。
- **主要生词**：大学、留学、公立、私立、学院、教学、招收、海外、留学生。
- **主要语言点**：没问题，是……还是……，表示概数的"多"。
- **文化小常识**：中国的高等教育。

一 看图讨论 Look at the picture and discuss

1. 下图的大学在哪儿？ Where is the university in the picture below?
2. 你听说过这所大学吗？ Have you heard of this university?

二 课文 Text

听录音回答问题 Listen to the recording and answer the following questions.

1. 马文问了些什么？What did Ma Wen ask?
2. 王老师是怎么回答的？How did Ms. Wang answer him?

Nín néng jièshào yíxiàr Jìnán Dàxué ma
您能介绍一下儿暨南大学吗 4-1

Mǎ Wén: Wǒ xiǎng qù Zhōngguó liúxué, nín néng jièshào yíxià
马 文： 我想去中国留学，您能介绍一下儿

Jìnán Dàxué ma?
暨南大学吗？

Wáng lǎoshī: Méi wèntí.
王 老师： 没问题。

Mǎ Wén: Tā shì gōnglì dàxué háishi sīlì dàxué?
马 文： 它是公立大学还是私立大学？

Wáng lǎoshī: Shì gōnglì dàxué.
王 老师： 是公立大学。

Mǎ Wén: Jìnán Dàxué yǒu duō dà?
马 文： 暨南大学有多大？

Wáng lǎoshī: Xiànzài yǒu sānshíqī gè xuéyuàn, zài xiào xuéshēng yígòng yǒu
王 老师： 现在有三十七个学院，在校学生一共有

		sìwàn duō rén.
		四万 多 人。

Mǎ Wén:	Xuéxiào de jiàoxué zhìliàng zěnmeyàng?
马 文:	学校 的 教学 质量 怎么样？

Wáng lǎoshī:	Jiàoxué zhìliàng hěn hǎo, shì Zhōngguó dì-yī suǒ zhāoshōu
王 老师:	教学 质量 很 好，是 中国 第一 所 招收

	hǎiwài liúxuéshēng de dàxué.
	海外 留学生 的 大学。

Mǎ Wén:	Xièxie!
马 文:	谢谢！

三 生词 New words 4-2

1.	暨南大学	专有名词	Jìnán Dàxué	Ji'nan University
	大学	名词	dàxué	university
2.	留学	动词	liúxué	study abroad
3.	公立	形容词	gōnglì	public
4.	还是	连词	háishi	or
5.	私立	形容词	sīlì	private
6.	学院	名词	xuéyuàn	school (of a university), college
7.	在校		zài xiào	in school
8.	万	数词	wàn	ten thousand
9.	教学	动词	jiàoxué	teach

10. 所	量词	suǒ	*a measure word for universities, schools, hospitals, etc.*
11. 招收	动词	zhāoshōu	enroll, recruit
12. 海外	名词	hǎiwài	overseas
13. 留学生	名词	liúxuéshēng	overseas student

四 主要语言点 Main language points

1 没问题。

本课对话中的"没问题"表示完全可以做到、一点儿也不麻烦。交际中，"没问题"可用于同意别人提出的请求、命令等。例如：

"没问题" in the dialogue of this lesson means that something can be done without any trouble. In communication, it can be used to agree to other people's requests, orders, etc. For example:

（1）A：你可以教我学汉语吗？
　　　B：没问题。

（2）A：我可以借一下儿你的笔记本吗？
　　　B：没问题。

（3）A：你明天能做完作业吗？
　　　B：没问题。

（4）A：你能帮我买一点儿水果吗？
　　　B：没问题。

▶ 视频：4.1 没问题。

❷ 它是公立大学还是私立大学?

"是……还是……"是一种选择疑问句,即提出两个或两个以上的答案供对方选择的一种疑问句。其中,第一个"是"字有时可以省略。例如:

"是……还是……" is an alternative question, that is, a question that proposes two or more answers for the other party to choose from. "是" that appears first can sometimes be omitted. For example:

(1) 你是今天走还是明天走?
(2) 他是你的同学还是男朋友?
(3) 你是喝茶还是喝牛奶?
(4) 我们今天去还是明天去?

▶ 视频: 4.2 它是公立大学还是私立大学?

❸ 在校学生一共有四万多人。

"多"用于"数词+多(+量词)"格式中时,表示一个大概的数,意思是实际的数量大于"多"前面的数量,但是超过的量小于"多"前的一个数量单位。例如:

"多" indicates an approximate number when it is used in "number + 多 (+ measure word)", meaning the actual number is larger than that before "多", but the exceeding number is less than a unit of quantity before "多". For example:

(1) 我们学院有五千多人。(实际总人数大于五千,但是多出的量小于一"千",即实际总人数大于五千且小于六千。)
(2) 世界上有两百多个国家。(实际国家总数大于两百,但是多出的量小于一"百",即实际国家总数大于两百且小于三百。)

（3）我们系有九十多位老师。（实际老师总数大于九十，但是多出的量小于一"十"，即实际老师总数大于九十且小于一百。）

▶ 视频：4.2 它是公立大学还是私立大学？

五 文化小常识 General knowledge of culture

中国的高等教育

中国一直高度重视高等教育。经过不断改革和调整，中国高等教育的办学规模不断发展，人才培养层次日趋合理，专业结构设置更加优化，办学质量明显提高。2023年，中国共有十多所大学进入QS（Quacquarelli Symonds）世界大学排名TOP 100。世界各地来中国留学的人数逐年攀升。

Higher Education in China

China has always attached great importance to higher education. After continuous reform and adjustment, its higher education has been constantly developing in scale, the talent cultivation at various levels has become increasingly reasonable, the professional structure setting has been more optimized, and the quality of education has been significantly improved. In 2023, more than ten Chinese universities entered the world's Top 100 QS (Quacquarelli Symonds) universities. The number of students studying in China from all over the world has been increasing year by year.

六 练习与实践 Exercises and practice

1 听录音，选择你听到的音，然后朗读下面的拼音。 4-3

Listen to the recording and choose the pronunciation you hear, then read the following Pinyin aloud.

（1）院 — 员　yuàn　yuán
（2）高 — 考　gāo　kǎo
（3）所 — 左　suǒ　zuǒ

（4）兰 — 南　lán　nán
（5）抄 — 招　chāo　zhāo
（6）公 — 空　gōng　kōng

（7）你 — 立　nǐ　lì
（8）暨 — 系　jì　xì
（9）私 — 四　sī　sì

（10）留学 — 九月　liúxué　jiǔ yuè
（11）红梨 — 公立　hóng lí　gōnglì

（12）字体 — 私立　zìtǐ　sīlì
（13）学院 — 月圆　xuéyuàn　yuè yuán

（14）全球 — 甜酒　quánqiú　tián jiǔ
（15）招手 — 招收　zhāoshǒu　zhāoshōu

2 朗读下面的句子，注意语调、语气和重音。

Read the following sentences aloud, paying attention to the intonation, tone and stress.

（1）您能介绍一下儿暨南大学吗？

（2）没问题。

（3）它是公立大学还是私立大学？

（4）它是公立大学。

（5）暨南大学有多大？

（6）现在有三十七个学院，在校学生一共有四万多人。

（7）学校的教学质量怎么样？

3 替换练习。
Substitution drills.

（1）<u>学校的教学质量怎么样</u>？

这种茶叶的
华为手机的
这台电脑的

（2）<u>暨南大学是公立大学还是私立大学</u>？

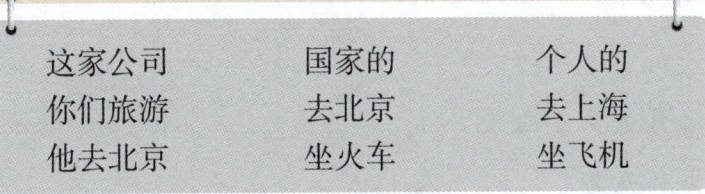

这家公司	国家的	个人的
你们旅游	去北京	去上海
他去北京	坐火车	坐飞机

（3）<u>这所大学有四万多学生</u>。

这家公司的员工有三千　　名
他这次考了九十　　　　　分
这件衣服要八百　　　　　块

4 选词填空。
Choose the right words to fill in the blanks.

是……还是……　　多

（1）她＿＿＿＿美国人＿＿＿＿英国人？

（2）她＿＿＿＿老师＿＿＿＿学生？

（3）今天_____星期四_____星期五？

（4）他写了八百_____字。

5 完成下面的对话，然后和同学一起表演对话的内容。
Complete the following dialogues, then act them out with your classmates.

（1）A：你们旅游_____去北京_____去上海？

　　B：去上海。

　　A：你们_____明天走_____后天走？

　　B：我们后天走。

（2）A：你可以给我介绍一下儿你们的学校吗？

　　B：_____。

　　A：你们学校有多少学生呢？

　　B：现在一共有五万_____人。

（3）A：你的口语考了多少？

　　B：考了八十_____分。

（4）A：今天买东西花（huā）了多少钱？

　　B：一共花了一千_____块。

（5）A：我能用一下儿你的汉语词典（cídiǎn）吗？

　　B：_____。

6 用下面的词语介绍一下儿你自己在读的大学或者喜欢的大学。
Introduce the university you study at or you are fond of with the following words.

公立　　私立　　排名　　学院　　在校　　多　　教学质量

7 看视频，先回答问题，然后和同学一起表演视频的内容。
Watch the video and answer the questions. Then act out the video with your classmates.

（1）这所大学有多少个学院？

（2）这所大学有多少学生？

▶ 视频：4.3 暨南大学有多大？

8 汉字练习：看汉字笔画笔顺动态图，并跟着书写。
Practice Chinese characters: Look at the animated illustrations of the strokes and the order of strokes of the following characters, and then write them down.

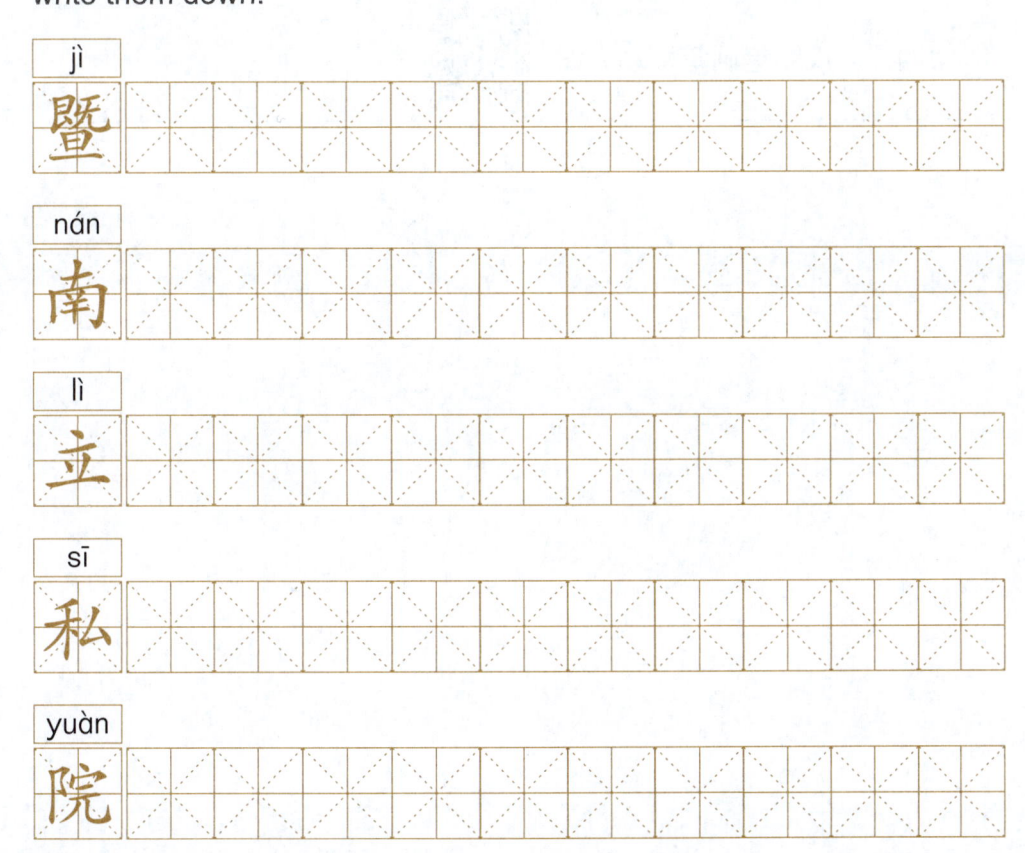

jì
暨

nán
南

lì
立

sī
私

yuàn
院

43

suǒ
所

zhāo
招

hǎi
海

wài
外

第四课　汉字笔画笔顺动态图

第五课 Lesson 5

Zhōngyī yǒu shénme tèdiǎn ne
中医有什么特点呢

重点提示

- **交际功能**：介绍中医。
- **主要生词**：刚才、看病、医学、理论、方法、治疗、特别、适合、慢性病、各、种、疑难杂症、重视、人体、部分、关系。
- **主要语言点**：代词"哪些"，代词"各"，量词"种"，副词"最"。
- **文化小常识**：中医药在全球的发展。

一 看图讨论 Look at the picture and discuss

1. 你知道图中展示的是什么工作吗？ Do you know what job is in the picture?
2. 你了解它的特点吗？ Do you know its features?

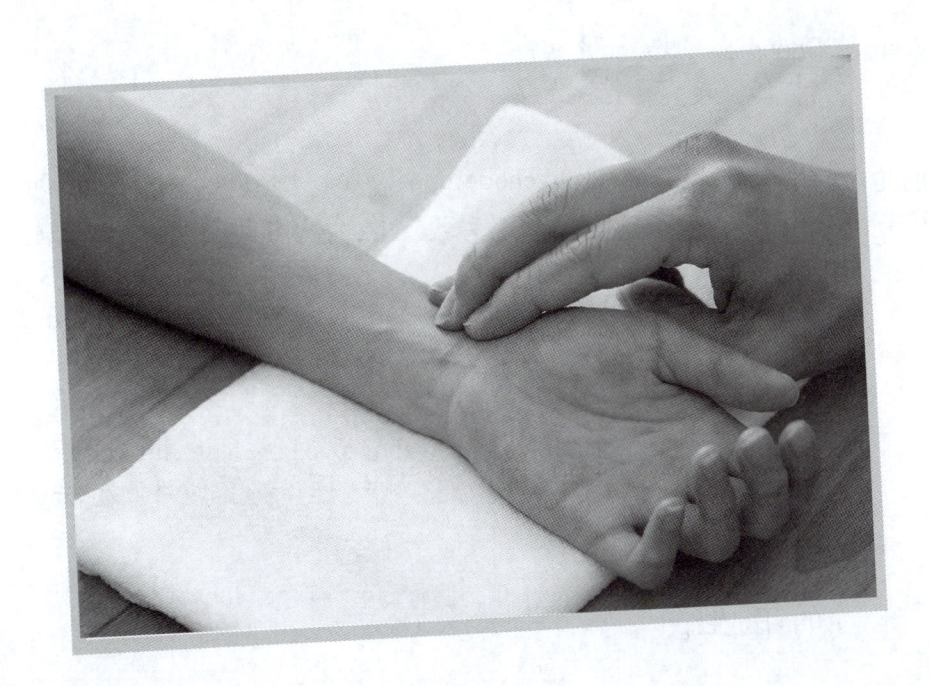

45

二 课文 Text

听录音回答问题 Listen to the recording and answer the following questions.

1. 李安平看的什么医生？ What doctor did Li Anping see?
2. 马文问了李安平哪些问题？ What questions did Ma Wen ask Li Anping?
3. 李安平是怎么回答这些问题的？ How did Li Anping answer these questions?

中医有什么特点呢 5-1
Zhōngyī yǒu shénme tèdiǎn ne

Mǎ Wén / 马文：
Gāngcái gěi nǐ kànbìng de shì shénme yīshēng?
刚才给你看病的是什么医生？

Lǐ Ānpíng / 李安平：
Shì zhōngyī.
是中医。

Mǎ Wén / 马文：
Shénme shì zhōngyī ne?
什么是中医呢？

Lǐ Ānpíng / 李安平：
Zhōngyī shì Zhōngguó chuántǒng yīxué de jiǎnchēng, jiù shì yòng Zhōngguó de chuántǒng yīxué lǐlùn hé fāngfǎ zhìbìng de yì zhǒng yīxué, yě kěyǐ zhǐ yòng zhè zhǒng yīxué lǐlùn hé fāngfǎ zhìbìng de yīshēng.
中医是中国传统医学的简称，就是用中国的传统医学理论和方法治病的一种医学，也可以指用这种医学理论和方法治病的医生。

第五课 ● 中医有什么特点呢

Mǎ Wén: Zhōngyī kěyǐ zhìliáo nǎxiē bìng ne?
马 文： 中医 可以 治疗 哪些 病 呢？

Lǐ Ānpíng: Zhōngyī kěyǐ zhìliáo hěn duō bìng, tèbié shìhé zhìliáo yìxiē mànxìng-
李安平： 中医 可以 治疗 很 多 病，特别 适合 治疗 一些 慢性

bìng hé gèzhǒng yínán zázhèng.
病 和 各种 疑难 杂症。

Mǎ Wén: Zhōngyī yǒu nǎxiē tèdiǎn ne?
马 文： 中医 有 哪些 特点 呢？

Lǐ Ānpíng: Zhōngyī de zuì dà tèdiǎn shì tā de zhěngtǐ guānniàn, jiù shì zhòngshì
李安平： 中医 的 最大 特点 是 它 的 整体 观念，就是 重视

réntǐ gè bùfen de guānxì.
人体 各 部分 的 关系。

三 》 生 词 New words 5-2

1. 刚才	名词	gāngcái	just now
2. 看病	动词	kànbìng	see a doctor
3. 医学	名词	yīxué	medicine, medical science
4. 理论	名词	lǐlùn	theory
5. 方法	名词	fāngfǎ	method
6. 指	动词	zhǐ	indicate
7. 治疗	动词	zhìliáo	cure, treat (a disease)
8. 哪些	代词	nǎxiē	which, what
9. 特别	副词	tèbié	especially

47

10. 适合	动词	shìhé	fit, suit
11. 慢性病	名词	mànxìngbìng	chronic disease
12. 各种	代词	gèzhǒng	all kinds of
各	代词	gè	all, every
种	量词	zhǒng	kind, type
13. 疑难杂症		yínán zázhèng	miscellaneous cases of illness that are hard to diagnose and cure
14. 最	副词	zuì	to the highest/lowest degree
15. 整体	名词	zhěngtǐ	entirety
16. 观念	名词	guānniàn	concept, idea
17. 重视	动词	zhòngshì	attach importance to
18. 人体	名词	réntǐ	human body
19. 部分	名词	bùfen	part
20. 关系	名词	guānxì	relationship

四 主要语言点 Main language points

1 中医可以治疗哪些病呢？

"哪些"是疑问代词，用于询问所指的对象为两个或两个以上的人或者事物时。例如：

"哪些" is an interrogative pronoun, which is used to inquire two or more people or things. For example:

（1）哪些同学迟到了？

（2）你喜欢吃哪些水果？

（3）我们班的同学来自哪些国家？
（4）大家还有哪些词不懂（dǒng）吗？

▶ 视频：5.1 中医可以治疗哪些病呢？

❷ 中医可以治疗很多病，特别适合治疗一些慢性病和各种疑难杂症。

"各"是一个指示代词，指代某个范围内的所有个体，常用在量词或者名词前面。例如：

"各" is a demonstrative pronoun, referring to all the individuals within a certain range. It is often used before a measure word or a noun. For example:

（1）各种书都可以看看。
（2）各种水果都好吃。
（3）各个班都有汉语课。
（4）各位同学请注意！
（5）各学校要做好留学生教学工作！

▶ 视频：5.1 中医可以治疗哪些病呢？

"种"是一个集合量词，用于内部一致而对外有区别的一组事物。例如：
"种" is a collective measure word, which is used for a group of things that are consistent internally but different externally. For example:

（6）书店有很多种书。
（7）这里有很多种水果。
（8）校园里有很多种花。

3 中医的最大特点是它的整体观念。

"最"是一个程度副词,表示在同类事物中或某方面占第一位。例如:
The adverb of degree "最" means being the first among things of the same kind or in a certain aspect. For example:

(1)小王这次考得最好。
(2)她最大的优点是关心朋友。
(3)那个题最难。
(4)这种水果最便宜。

五 文化小常识 General knowledge of culture

中医药在全球的发展

现在,中医药已传播到全球196个国家和地区,受到越来越多的国家和地区的认可和欢迎。据世界卫生组织统计,113个世卫组织成员国认可针灸等中医药诊疗方式。中医药教育在国外的发展非常迅速,国外有不少正规大学设有中医系或中医专业,如泰国华侨崇圣大学、澳大利亚中华针灸学院、英国伦敦中医学院、奥地利时珍中医大学、美洲中医学院等。

The Development of Traditional Chinese Medicine in the World

Nowadays, traditional Chinese medicine (TCM) has spread to 196 countries and regions worldwide, receiving recognition and welcome from more and more countries and regions. According to the statistics of the World Health Organization,

113 member countries of the World Health Organization recognize the diagnosis and treatment of traditional Chinese medicine such as acupuncture. The education of traditional Chinese medicine has enjoyed rapid development abroad. Many foreign universities have TCM departments or specialties, such as Huachiew Chalermprakiet University in Thailand, Australian College of Chinese Acupuncture and Moxibustion, London College of Traditional Chinese Medicine, UK., Austria Shizhen University of Traditional Chinese Medicine in Austria, and American College of Traditional Chinese Medicine.

六 练习与实践 Exercises and practice

1 听录音，选择你听到的音，然后朗读下面的拼音。 5-3
Listen to the recording and choose the pronunciation you hear, then read the following Pinyin aloud.

（1）吃 chī — 治 zhì
（2）平 píng — 病 bìng
（3）课 kè — 各 gè
（4）种 zhǒng — 从 cóng
（5）干柴 gānchái — 刚才 gāngcái
（6）治病 zhìbìng — 次品 cìpǐn
（7）治疗 zhìliáo — 十秒 shí miǎo
（8）转动 zhuàndòng — 传统 chuántǒng
（9）你们 nǐmen — 理论 lǐlùn
（10）方法 fāngfǎ — 看法 kànfǎ
（11）哪些 nǎxiē — 那些 nàxiē
（12）课题 kètí — 特别 tèbié
（13）十课 shí kè — 适合 shìhé
（14）慢性 mànxìng — 南京 Nánjīng

实用交际汉语 3
Practical Communicative Chinese

2 朗读下面的句子，注意语调、语气和停顿。
Read the following sentences aloud, paying attention to the tone, intonation and pause.

（1）刚才给你看病的是什么医生？

（2）什么是中医呢？

（3）中医是中国传统医学的简称，就是用中国的传统医学理论和方法治病的一种医学，也可以指用这种医学理论和方法治病的医生。

（4）中医可以治疗哪些病呢？

（5）中医可以治疗很多病，特别适合治疗一些慢性病和各种疑难杂症。

（6）中医有哪些特点呢？

（7）中医的最大特点是它的整体观念，就是重视人体各部分的关系。

3 替换练习。
Substitution drills.

（1）刚才给你看病的是什么医生？

你在和谁打电话
你去哪儿了
老师说了什么

（2）中医可以治疗哪些病呢？

你在学习	课程
中国有	有名的大学
北京有	好玩儿的地方

（3）中医可以治疗各种慢性病和疑难杂症。

在这里你可以学习	知识（zhīshi）
在图书馆你可以借	书
那个商店卖	水果

52

4 连词成句。
Arrange the words to make sentences.

（1）有 的 哪些 景点 那里 好玩儿

_____?

（2）谁 你 来 刚才 找

_____?

（3）特别 中医 各 治疗 种 适合 疑难杂症

_____。

（4）特点 中医 是 整体 的 最大 的 观念 它

_____。

（5）种 中医 治疗 多 可以 很 病

_____。

5 完成对话，然后和同学一起表演对话的内容。
Complete the following dialogues, then act them out with your classmates.

（1）A: _____你去了哪儿？

　　 B: _____我去了图书馆。

（2）A: 她_____做什么工作？

　　 B: 她很_____当汉语老师。

（3）A: 中国有_____有名的大学呢？

　　 B: 有很多，_____有名的有北京大学、清华大学等。

（4）A: 这里有什么水果？

　　 B: 这里有很多_____水果，_____水果都好吃。

实用交际汉语 3
Practical Communicative Chinese

❻ 用下面的词语介绍一下儿你自己国家的中医发展情况，包括中药的使用情况等。
Introduce the development of traditional Chinese medical science in your country, including the use of traditional Chinese medicine with the following words.

中医　中药　治疗　各　种　适合　慢性病　疑难杂症

❼ 看图，说一说中医的基本内容，包括它在治疗方式上的特点。
Look at the picture and talk about the basics of traditional Chinese medical science, including its treatment characteristics.

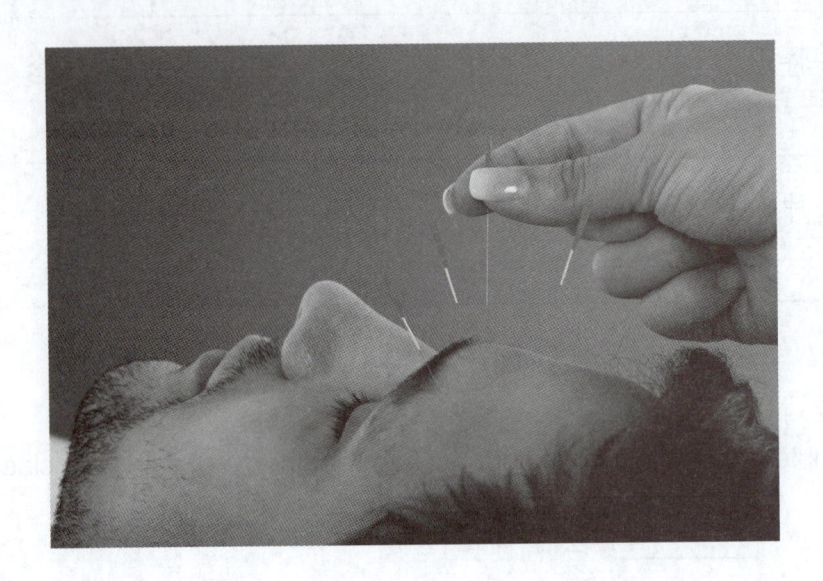

❽ 汉字练习：看汉字笔画笔顺动态图，并跟着书写。
Practice Chinese characters: Look at the animated illustrations of the strokes and the order of strokes of the following characters, and then write them down.

gāng
刚

第五课 中医有什么特点呢

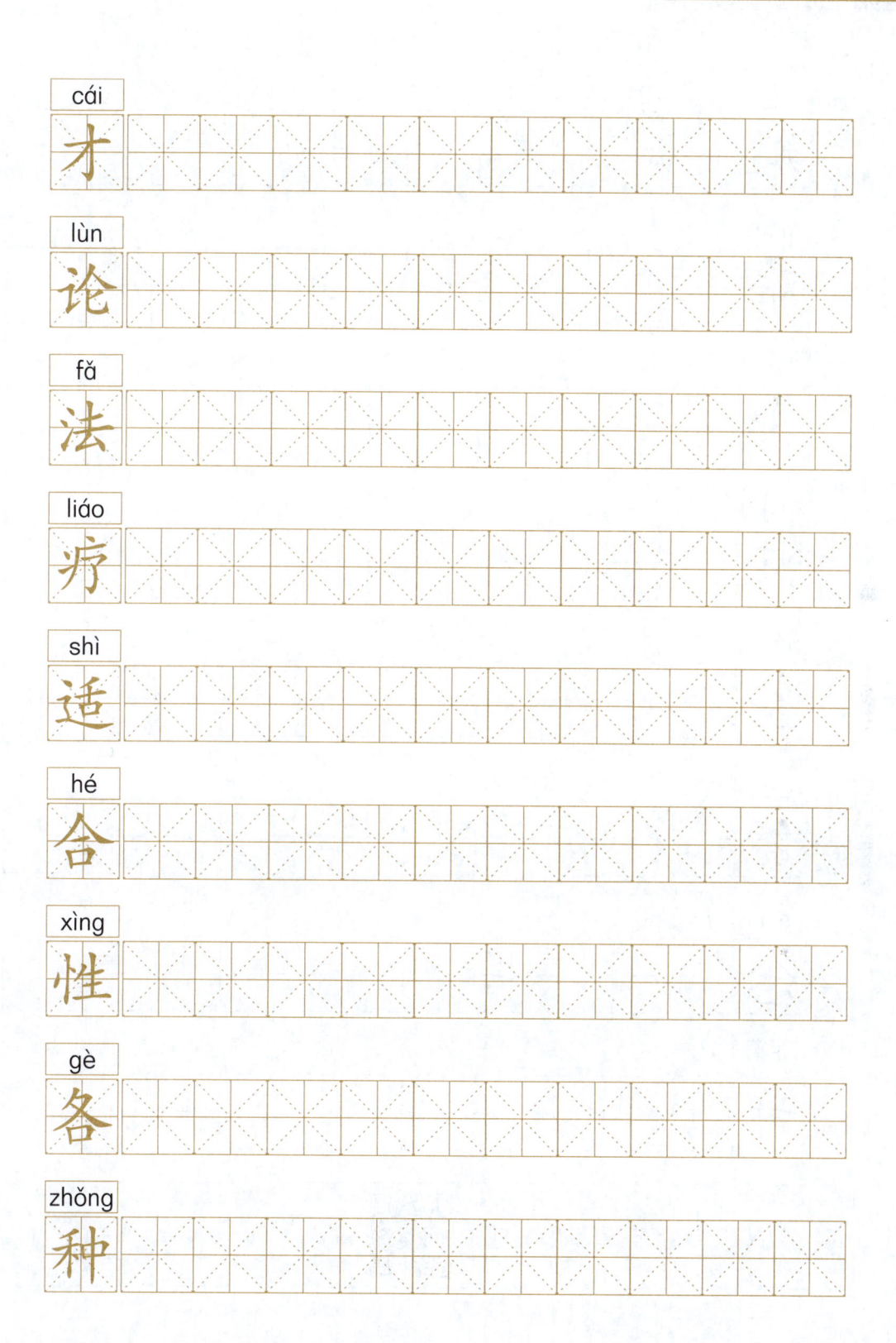

cái
才

lùn
论

fǎ
法

liáo
疗

shì
适

hé
合

xìng
性

gè
各

zhǒng
种

yí
疑

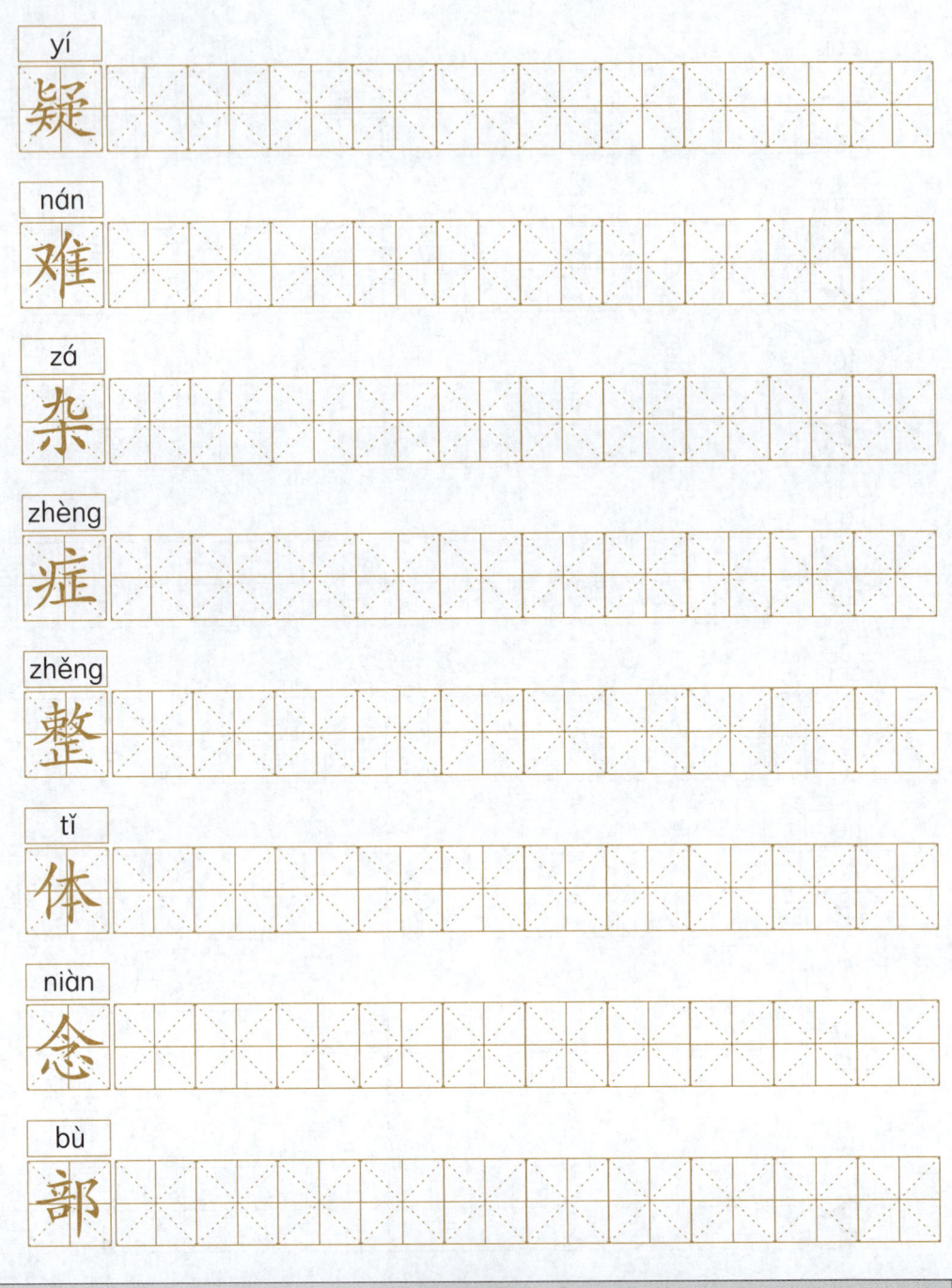

nán
难

zá
杂

zhèng
症

zhěng
整

tǐ
体

niàn
念

bù
部

第五课　汉字笔画笔顺动态图

第六课 Lesson 6

Hē chá yǒu shénme hǎochù ne
喝茶有什么好处呢

重点提示

- 交际功能：讨论喝茶的好处。
- 主要生词：好处、制作、茶叶、预防、疾病、身体、更、健康、有名、就、带、礼物。
- 主要语言点：副词"就"，再好不过。
- 文化小常识：喝茶的好处和注意事项。

一 看图讨论 Look at the picture and discuss

1. 下图是什么？你喝过吗？ What is in the picture below? Have you ever drunk it?
2. 你知道喝中国茶的好处吗？ Do you know the benefits of drinking Chinese tea?

57

二 课文 Text

听录音回答问题 Listen to the recording and answer the following questions.

1. 他们在谈论什么？ What are they talking about?
2. 李安平说到了哪些有名的中国茶？ What famous Chinese tea did Li Anping mention?
3. 马文准备带什么回国？ What is Ma Wen going to take back to his motherland?

Hē chá yǒu shénme hǎochù ne
喝茶有什么好处呢 6-1

Mǎ Wén: Hěn duō Zhōngguórén ài hē chá, shì ma?
马 文： 很多 中国人 爱喝茶，是吗？

Lǐ Ānpíng: Shìde, Zhōngguó shì shìjiè shang zuì zǎo zhìzuò cháyè de guójiā,
李安平： 是的，中国 是世界 上 最早 制作 茶叶的国家，

hē chá de rén yě zuì duō.
喝茶的人也最多。

Mǎ Wén: Hē chá yǒu shénme hǎochù ne?
马 文： 喝茶有什么 好处呢？

Lǐ Ānpíng: Hǎochù hěn duō, zuì dà de hǎochù shì yùfáng jíbìng, ràng shēntǐ
李安平： 好处 很多，最大的好处是预防 疾病，让 身体

gèng jiànkāng.
更 健康。

Mǎ Wén: Nǐ néng jièshào yìxiē yǒumíng de cháyè ma?
马 文： 你能 介绍一些 有名 的茶叶吗？

Lǐ Ānpíng: Zhōngguó yǒumíng de chá hěn duō, zhǔyào yǒu lóngjǐng、
李安平： 中国 有名 的 茶 很 多， 主要 有 龙井、

tiěguānyīn děng.
铁观音 等。

Mǎ Wén: Xièxie! Yǐhòu huí guó wǒ jiù dài xiē cháyè huí jiā.
马 文： 谢谢！以后 回 国 我 就 带 些 茶叶 回 家。

Lǐ Ānpíng: Nà shì zài hǎo búguò de lǐwù le!
李安平： 那 是 再 好 不 过 的 礼物 了！

三 生词 New words 6–2

1. 好处	名词	hǎochù	benefit
2. 世界	名词	shìjiè	world
3. 早	形容词	zǎo	early
4. 制作	动词	zhìzuò	make
5. 茶叶	名词	cháyè	tea
6. 预防	动词	yùfáng	prevent
7. 疾病	名词	jíbìng	disease
8. 让	动词	ràng	let
9. 身体	名词	shēntǐ	physical constitution, health
10. 更	副词	gèng	more
11. 健康	形容词	jiànkāng	healthy

12. 有名	形容词	yǒumíng	famous
13. 龙井	名词	lóngjǐng	Longjing, a famous Chinese tea
14. 铁观音	名词	tiěguānyīn	Tieguanyin, a famous Chinese tea
15. 就	副词	jiù	just
16. 带	动词	dài	take
17. 再好不过		zài hǎo búguò	be perfect
18. 礼物	名词	lǐwù	gift, present

四 主要语言点 Main language points

1 以后回国我就带些茶叶回家。

这里的"就"是一个副词，用于"……（，）就＋动词"格式，表示承接上文，得出结论。例如：

The adverb "就" is used in the structure "……（，）就 + verb", which indicates making a conclusion based on what was mentioned previously. For example:

（1）没有车，我就不去了。
（2）我有时间就去看他。
（3）明天的晚会（wǎnhuì）你有事就不用来。
（4）今天的作业我做完了就发给你。

▶ 视频：6.1 以后回国我就带些茶叶回家。

2 那是再好不过的礼物了!

"再好不过"的意思是说话人认为某件事或某种情况是最好的,没有比说的这件事或这种情况更好的了。例如:

"再好不过" means that the speaker thinks that something or a certain situation is the best, and there is nothing better than this matter or this situation mentioned. For example:

> (1) 你去找他是再好不过的了!
> (2) 这是再好不过的消息了!
> (3) 茶叶是再好不过的礼物了!

▶ 视频:6.1 以后回国我就带些茶叶回家。

五 文化小常识 General knowledge of culture

喝茶的好处和注意事项

坚持喝茶,可以防治口腔炎、咽喉炎,防止血压上升,同时有增强心脏功能、提神醒脑、消除疲劳、提高思维和记忆能力等多种作用。不过,大家喝茶时要注意:(1)不要喝太浓的茶;(2)不要喝太烫的茶;(3)不要喝过夜的茶;(4)喝牛奶的同时不要喝茶;(5)吃药之后也不要喝茶。部

分人群不宜喝茶，比如失眠、结核病、心脏病、胃病等患者，怀孕妇女和婴幼儿等。

The Benefits and Precautions of Drinking Tea

Persisting in drinking tea can prevent and cure stomatitis and pharyngitis, prevent blood pressure from rising, and also enhance heart function, refresh one's mind, eliminate fatigue, and improve thinking and memory abilities. However, when drinking tea, people should pay attention to: (1) Don't drink too strong tea; (2) Don't drink too hot tea; (3) Don't drink tea overnight; (4) Don't drink tea while drinking milk; (5) Don't drink tea after taking medicine. Some people should not drink tea, such as patients with insomnia, tuberculosis, heart disease, or stomach disorder, and pregnant women or infants.

六 练习与实践 Exercises and practice

1 听录音，选择你听到的音，然后朗读下面的拼音。 6-3
Listen to the recording and choose the pronunciation you hear, then read the following Pinyin aloud.

（1）就 jiù — 休 xiū　　（2）太 tài — 带 dài　　（3）最 zuì — 岁 suì

（4）制作 zhìzuò — 吃错 chīcuò　　（5）告诉 gàosu — 好处 hǎochù

（6）预防 yùfáng — 夕阳 xīyáng　　（7）疾病 jíbìng — 七瓶 qī píng

　　　　shēntǐ　　　zhēnlǐ　　　　　　　　xiànchǎng　jiànkāng
（8）身体 — 真理　　　　　（9）现场 — 健康

　　　　yǒumíng　　jiǔ líng　　　　　　　　nǐ fù　　lǐwù
（10）有名 — 九零　　　　　（11）你付 — 礼物

2 朗读下面的句子，注意语调、语气和停顿。
Read the following sentences aloud, paying attention to the tone, intonation and pause.

（1）很多中国人爱喝茶，是吗？
（2）中国是世界上最早制作茶叶的国家。
（3）喝茶有什么好处呢？
（4）你能介绍一些有名的茶叶吗？
（5）以后回国我就带些茶叶回家。
（6）那是再好不过的礼物了！

3 连线组成短语，并读一读。
Match the words to make phrases and read them.

爱　　　　　　　健康
制作　　　　　　喝茶
预防　　　　　　疾病
身体　　　　　　茶叶
带　　　　　　　礼物

4 替换练习。
Substitution drills.

（1）<u>喝茶</u>最<u>大</u>的<u>好处</u>是什么？

早睡（shuì）	大	好处
马文	喜欢	运动
学口语	重要（zhòngyào）	方法

（2）<u>喝茶</u>最<u>大</u>的<u>好处</u>是<u>预防疾病，让身体更健康</u>。

早睡	大	好处	身体可以得到充分（chōngfèn）的休息（xiūxi）
马文	喜欢	运动	踢足球
学口语	重要	方法	多听多说

（3）我<u>有时间</u>就<u>给你打电话</u>。

毕业了	去当汉语老师
如果见到她	告诉她
没有课	参加比赛

5 看视频，先回答问题，然后和同学一起表演视频的内容。
Watch the video and answer the questions. Then act out the video with your classmates.

（1）男的准备以后带什么礼物回国？
（2）女的觉得这种礼物怎么样？

▶ 视频：6.1 以后回国我就带些茶叶回家。

6 用下列词语介绍一下儿自己和家人爱喝的茶，包括这些茶的产地、喝茶的好处等。

Introduce the tea you and your family like with the following words, including the origins and benefits of the tea.

龙井　铁观音　预防　疾病　有名　就　礼物　最　世界上

7 汉字练习：看汉字笔画笔顺动态图，并跟着书写。

Practice Chinese characters: Look at the animated illustrations of the strokes and the order of strokes of the following characters, and then write them down.

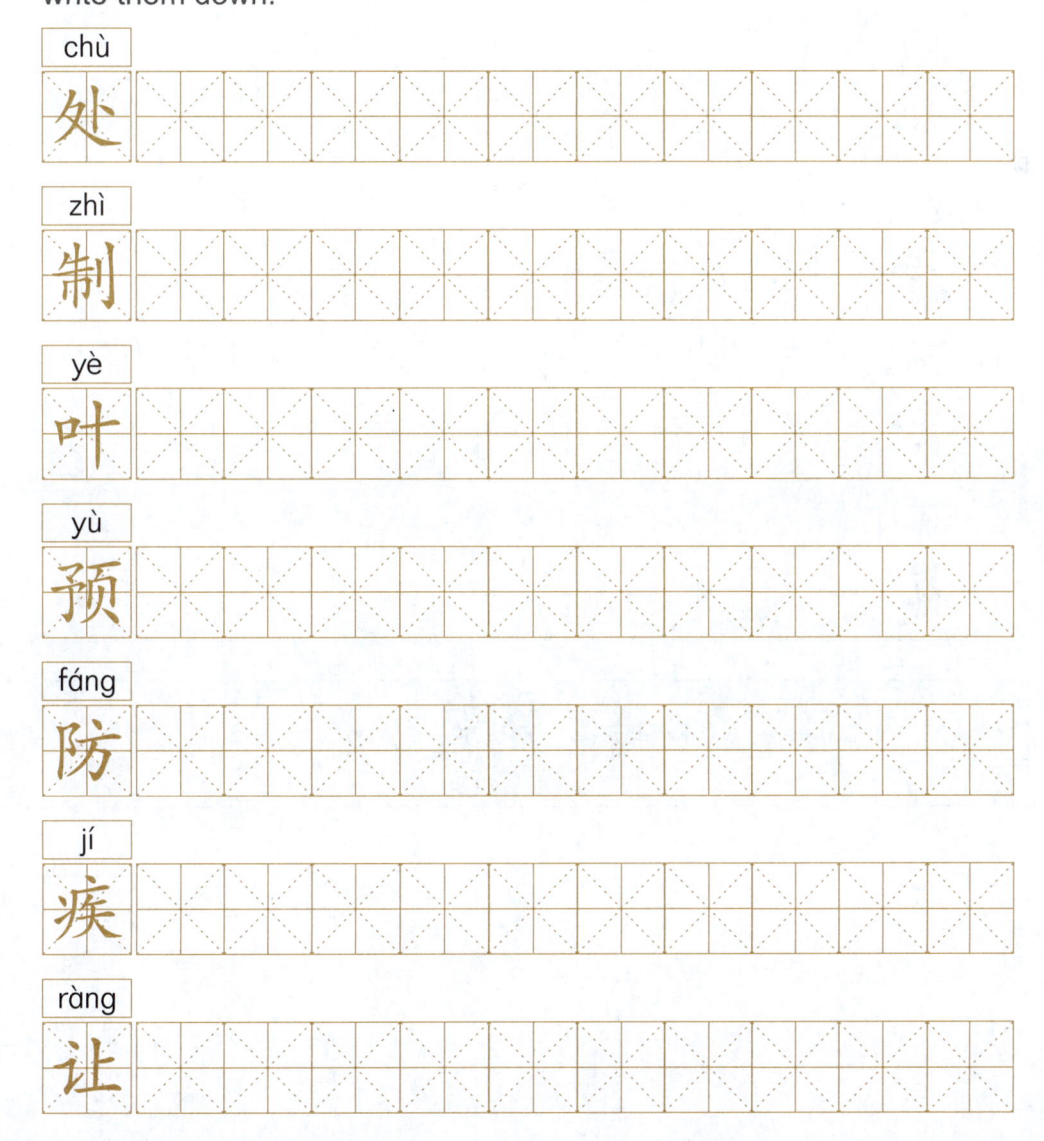

| chù |
| 处 |

| zhì |
| 制 |

| yè |
| 叶 |

| yù |
| 预 |

| fáng |
| 防 |

| jí |
| 疾 |

| ràng |
| 让 |

65

gèng
更

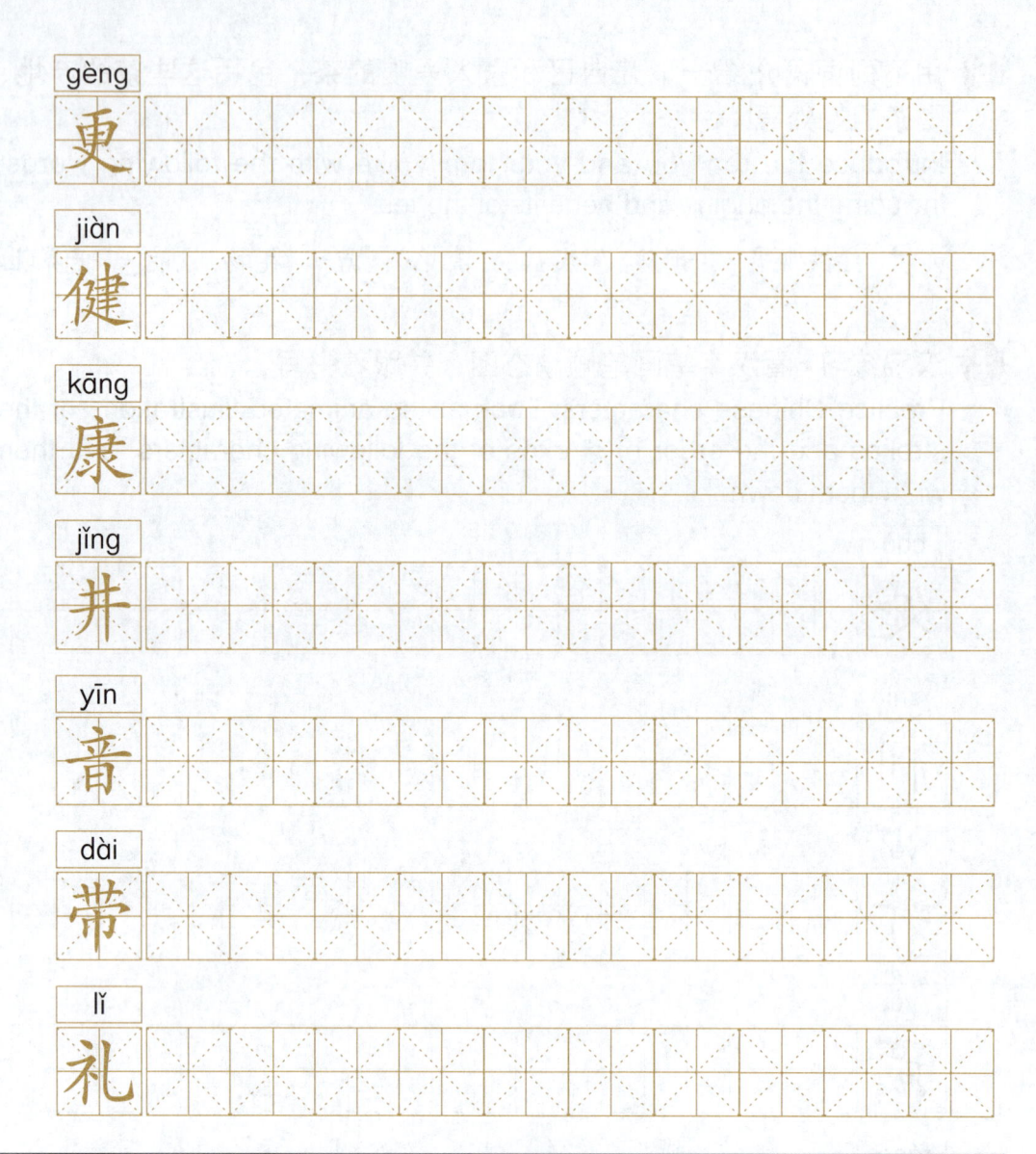

jiàn
健

kāng
康

jǐng
井

yīn
音

dài
带

lǐ
礼

第六课　汉字笔画笔顺动态图

交际项目三
说　明

第七课 Lesson 7

Wǒ xiǎng cānjiā HSK péixùnbān
我想参加 HSK 培训班

重点提示

- 交际功能：咨询培训班。
- 主要生词：培训班、需要、帮忙、报、填、表。
- 主要语言点：开始+动词，时间词语+就。
- 文化小常识：HSK。

一 看图讨论 Look at the picture and discuss

1. 下图可能是什么内容的培训班呢？ What kind of training course might the following picture be?
2. 你参加过这样的培训班吗？ Have you ever participated in such a training course?

二 › 课文 Text

听录音回答问题 Listen to the recording and answer the following questions.

1. 马文想做什么？ What did Ma Wen want to do?
2. 女的告诉了他一些什么？ What did the woman tell him?

我想参加HSK培训班 7-1
Wǒ xiǎng cānjiā HSK péixùnbān

老师 lǎoshī：你好，这里是汉语培训中心，需要帮忙吗？
Nǐ hǎo, zhèlǐ shì Hànyǔ Péixùn Zhōngxīn, xūyào bāngmáng ma?

马文 Mǎ Wén：你好，你们有HSK培训班吗？
Nǐ hǎo, nǐmen yǒu HSK péixùnbān ma?

老师 lǎoshī：有，我们有晚间班和周末班两种。你想报哪种？
Yǒu, wǒmen yǒu wànjiānbān hé zhōumòbān liǎng zhǒng. Nǐ xiǎng bào nǎ zhǒng?

马文 Mǎ Wén：我想参加周末班，怎么报名呢？
Wǒ xiǎng cānjiā zhōumòbān, zěnme bàomíng ne?

老师 lǎoshī：好的。请你填一下儿报名表。
Hǎo de. Qǐng nǐ tián yíxiàr bàomíngbiǎo.

马文 Mǎ Wén：什么时候开始上课呢？
Shénme shíhou kāishǐ shàngkè ne?

69

lǎoshī: Xià ge xīngqīliù jiù kāishǐ shàngkè.
老 师：下个星期六就开始上课。

Mǎ Wén: Xièxie!
马 文：谢谢！

lǎoshī: Bú kèqi!
老 师：不客气！

三 生词 New words 🔊 7-2

1. 培训班	名词	péixùnbān	training course
培训	动词	péixùn	train
2. 汉语培训中心	专有名词	Hànyǔ Péixùn Zhōngxīn	Chinese Language Training Centre
中心	名词	zhōngxīn	centre
3. 需要	动词	xūyào	need
4. 帮忙	动词	bāngmáng	help
5. 晚间班	名词	wǎnjiānbān	night class
6. 周末班	名词	zhōumòbān	weekend class
7. 报	动词	bào	sign up
8. 填	动词	tián	fill

9. 报名表	名词	bàomíngbiǎo	registration form
表	名词	biǎo	form, table

四 主要语言点 Main language points

1 什么时候开始上课呢？

这句中的"开始"是一个动词，用于"开始 + 动词"格式时，表示动作开始发生。例如：

"开始" in this sentence is a verb. It indicates the beginning of an action when it is used in the pattern "开始 + verb". For example:

（1）我们明天开始考试。
（2）他们下个星期开始比赛。
（3）大家现在开始讨论（tǎolùn）。

▶ 视频：7.1 什么时候开始上课呢？

2 下个星期六就开始上课。

这句中的"就"是一个副词，用在表示时间的词语后，表示说话人认为说话的时间距离某个动作发生或某种情况出现的时间很短。例如：

"就" in this sentence is an adverb. It is used after the words of time, indicating that the speaker thinks that the time from the time of speaking to the occurrence of an action or a situation is very short. For example:

（1）我们五分钟后就出发。（说话人认为说话的时间距离出发的时间很短）

（2）学校下个月就放假。（说话人认为说话的时间距离放假的时间很短）

（3）你们还有一年就毕业了。（说话人认为说话的时间距离毕业的时间很短）

▶ 视频：7.1 什么时候开始上课呢？

五 文化小常识 General knowledge of culture

HSK

HSK 的全称是"中文水平考试"，是一项国际中文能力标准化考试，主要考查第一语言不是中文的考生在生活、学习和工作中运用中文进行交际的能力。HSK 共分九个等级，其中 HSK（七~九级）已于 2022 年底推出，考试形式包括纸笔考试和网络考试两种。HSK 成绩已经成为世界各国朋友留学中国、申请来华留学奖学金的必备条件。越来越多的国家政府部门和跨国企业把 HSK 成绩作为员工招聘、升职和加薪的重要依据。

HSK

HSK is the Pinyin abbreviation of "Chinese Proficiency Test", which is an international standardised Chinese proficiency test. It examines the Chinese proficiency of non-native candidates when they communicate in their life, study and work in Chinese. HSK is divided into 9 levels, among which HSK (Levels 7-9) were launched at the end of 2022, and the examination forms include paper-based examination and online examination. HSK scores have become a prerequisite for people around the world to study in China and apply for scholarships to study in China. More and more national government departments and multinational enterprises regard HSK scores as an important basis for employee recruitment, promotion and salary increase.

六 练习与实践 Exercises and practice

1 听录音，选择你听到的音，然后朗读下面的拼音。 🔊 7-3

Listen to the recording and choose the pronunciation you hear, then read the following Pinyin aloud.

（1）跑 — 报
　　pǎo　bào

（2）班 — 饭
　　bān　fàn

（3）培训 — 背心
　　péixùn　bèixīn

（4）从新 — 中心
　　cóngxīn　zhōngxīn

（5）板房 — 帮忙
　　bǎnfáng　bāngmáng

（6）报名 — 保命
　　bàomíng　bǎomìng

（7）培训班 — 背心摊
　　péixùnbān　bèixīntān

（8）收录单 — 周末班
　　shōulùdān　zhōumòbān

实用交际汉语 3
Practical Communicative Chinese

2 朗读下面的句子，注意停顿和重音。
Read the following sentences aloud, paying attention to the pause and stress.

（1）这里是汉语培训中心，需要帮忙吗？
（2）你们有 HSK 培训班吗？
（3）我们有晚间班和周末班两种。
（4）请你填一下儿报名表。
（5）什么时候开始上课呢？
（6）下个星期六就开始上课。

3 连线组成短语，并读一读。
Match the words to make phrases and read them.

培训	时候
下个	表
开始	中心
填	星期六
什么	上课

4 替换练习。
Substitution drills.

（1）我们有<u>晚间</u>班和<u>周末</u>班两<u>种</u>班。

汉语交际	汉语阅读（yuèdú）	门课
商贸汉语	旅游汉语	个专业（zhuānyè）
课堂（kètáng）教学	网络教学	种形式（xíngshì）

第七课　我想参加 HSK 培训班

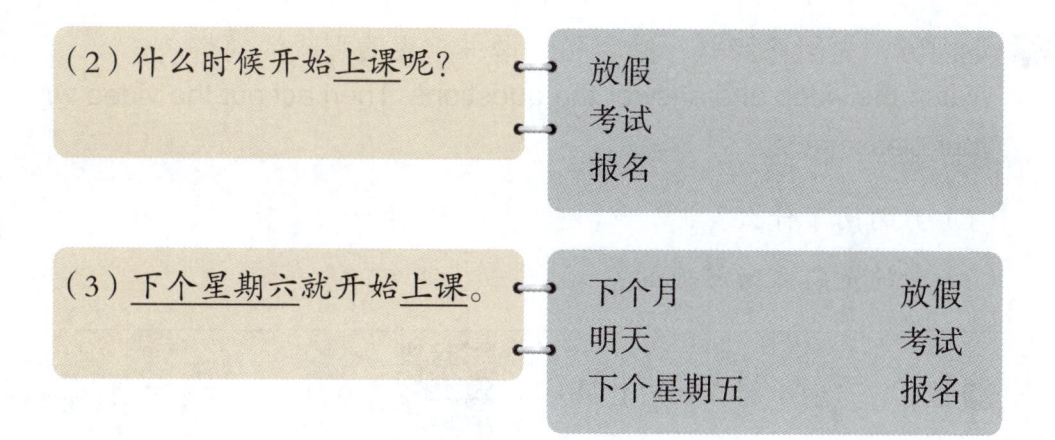

（2）什么时候开始上课呢？　　放假
　　　　　　　　　　　　　　考试
　　　　　　　　　　　　　　报名

（3）下个星期六就开始上课。　下个月　　　　　放假
　　　　　　　　　　　　　　明天　　　　　　考试
　　　　　　　　　　　　　　下个星期五　　　报名

5 完成对话，并和同学一起表演对话的内容。
Complete the following dialogues, then act them out with your classmates.

（1）A：请问有汉语培训班吗？

B：有。我们有晚间班和周末班两_____。

A：我想_____周末班。什么时候_____上课呢？

B：下个星期天_____开始上课。

（2）A：请问有太极拳_____班吗？

B：有。我们有大_____和小_____两种。

A：我想参加小_____。_____开始报名呢？

B：明天_____开始报名。

6 用下面的词语给同学介绍一下儿自己参加过的培训班，并说说报名的过程。

Introduce the training courses you have participated in to your classmates with the following words, and talk about the registration process.

培训班　　填　　报名　　就　　周末班　　晚间班　　开始　　上课

75

实用交际汉语 3
Practical Communicative Chinese

7 看视频，先回答问题，然后和同学一起表演视频的内容。
Watch the video and answer the questions. Then act out the video with your classmates.

（1）男的问了什么？

（2）女的是怎么回答他的？

▶ 视频：7.1 什么时候开始上课呢？

8 汉字练习：看汉字笔画笔顺动态图，并跟着书写。
Practice Chinese characters: Look at the animated illustrations of the strokes and the order of strokes of the following characters, and then write them down.

péi
培

xùn
训

bān
班

máng
忙

zhōu
周

第七课 我想参加 HSK 培训班

mò
末

bào
报

tián
填

第七课 汉字笔画笔顺动态图

第八课 Lesson 8

Wǒ kěyǐ jiè gèng cháng shíjiān ma
我可以借更长时间吗

重点提示

- 交际功能：在图书馆借书。
- 主要生词：借、本、多久、但是、办理、续借、手续。
- 主要语言点：副词"更"，连词"但是"。
- 文化小常识：图书馆。

一、看图讨论 Look at the picture and discuss

1. 这些小孩儿在做什么？ What are these children doing?
2. 他们可能会说什么呢？ What might they say?

二 课文 Text

听录音回答问题 Listen to the recording and answer the following questions.

1. 马文问了哪些问题？ What questions did Ma Wen ask?
2. 女的是怎么回答这些问题的？ How did the woman answer these questions?

Wǒ kěyǐ jiè gèng cháng shíjiān ma
我可以借更长时间吗 🔊 8-1

Mǎ Wén: Nín hǎo! Qǐngwèn wǒ kěyǐ jiè shū ma?
马 文： 您好！请问我可以借书吗？

guǎnlǐyuán: Dāngrán kěyǐ. Nǐ kěyǐ yòng zìjǐ de xuéshēngzhèng jiè shū.
管理员： 当然可以。你可以用自己的学生证借书。

Mǎ Wén: Wǒ yí cì kěyǐ jiè jǐ běn shū ne?
马 文： 我一次可以借几本书呢？

guǎnlǐyuán: Nǐ yí cì kěyǐ jiè shí běn shū.
管理员： 你一次可以借十本书。

Mǎ Wén: Tài hǎo le! Wǒ kěyǐ jiè duōjiǔ ne?
马 文： 太好了！我可以借多久呢？

guǎnlǐyuán: Liǎng gè xīngqī.
管理员： 两个星期。

Mǎ Wén: Kěyǐ jiè gèng cháng shíjiān ma?
马 文： 可以借更长时间吗？

79

实用交际汉语 3
Practical Communicative Chinese

guǎnlǐyuán: Kěyǐ, dànshì nǐ yào bànlǐ yíxiàr xùjiè shǒuxù.
管理员：可以，但是你要办理一下儿续借手续。

Mǎ Wén: Hǎo de, xièxie!
马 文：好的，谢谢！

三 生词 New words 8-2

1. 借	动词	jiè	borrow
2. 时间	名词	shíjiān	time
3. 本	量词	běn	a measure word for books
4. 多久	代词	duōjiǔ	how long
久	形容词	jiǔ	long, for a long time
5. 但是	连词	dànshì	but
6. 办理	动词	bànlǐ	handle, go through
7. 续借	动词	xùjiè	renew the loan of a library book
8. 手续	名词	shǒuxù	procedure

第八课　我可以借更长时间吗

四　主要语言点　Main language points

1 可以借更长时间吗？

这句中的"更"是一个程度副词，常用在形容词前面构成"更+形容词"的格式，表示比较，即某人或某事物的某一性质与某个参照体相比，程度还要高。例如：

"更" in this sentence is an adverb of degree, which is often used before an adjective to form the structure "更 + adjective". It is used to indicate comparison, that is, a certain property of someone or something is higher than that of the reference object. For example:

（1）他的哥哥很高，他更高。
（2）火车很快，飞机更快。
（3）一般（yìbān）可以借一个月，你可以借更长时间。
（4）马文的分数（fēnshù）很高，小李的分数更高。

▶ 视频：8.1 可以借更长时间吗？

2 但是你要办理一下儿续借手续。

"但是"是一个表示转折的连词，说话人用"但是"表示话题内容的转变，引出同上文相对立的意思或者补充上文的意思，表达的重点为"但是"后面的内容。例如：

"但是" is a conjunction indicating transition. The speaker uses it to indicate the change of the topic, leading to the opposite meaning or supplementing the meaning mentioned above. The expression focuses on the content after "但是". For example:

81

（1）你可以晚一点儿来，但是时间不能太长。

（2）大家可以进去，但是要有学生证。

（3）这里可以看书，但是不要说话。

（4）他可以参加，但是要提前报名。

▶ 视频：8.1 可以借更长时间吗？

五 》 文化小常识 General knowledge of culture

图书馆

　　图书馆是专门收集、整理、保存各种图书和资料的地方。我们可以去图书馆借书，也可以去那儿阅读各种报刊、资料。在现代信息社会里，我们还可以上各大图书馆的网站检索世界各地的最新科学资讯，下载各种学习资料。中国最大的图书馆是中国国家图书馆。大学里的图书馆更是学生们学习和研究的重要帮手。

Library

　　A library is a place where books and materials are collected, sorted and preserved. We can go to the library to borrow books and read various newspapers and magazines. In the modern information society, we can also search for the latest scientific information from all over the world and download various learning materials on the websites of major libraries. The largest library in China is the National Library of China. The library in universities provides much help in students' learning and research.

六 》 练习与实践 Exercises and practice

1 听录音，选择你听到的音，然后朗读下面的拼音。 8-3
Listen to the recording and choose the pronunciation you hear, then read the following Pinyin aloud.

（1）借 — 些　　　（2）知 — 次　　　（3）更 — 很
　　　jiè　xiē　　　　　zhī　cì　　　　　gèng　hěn

（4）自己 — 支持　　（5）干事 — 但是
　　　zìjǐ　zhīchí　　　　gànshi　dànshì

（6）帮你 — 办理　　（7）续借 — 去写
　　　bāng nǐ　bànlǐ　　　xùjiè　qù xiě

（8）手续 — 过去　　（9）更 长 — 肯 上
　　　shǒuxù　guòqù　　　gèng cháng　kěn shàng

2 朗读下面的句子，注意语调、语气和停顿。
Read the following sentences aloud, paying attention to the tone, intonation and pause.

（1）请问我可以借书吗？

（2）你可以用自己的学生证借书。

（3）我一次可以借几本书呢？

（4）你一次可以借十本书。

（5）我可以借多久呢？

（6）可以借更长时间吗？

（7）可以，但是你要办理一下儿续借手续。

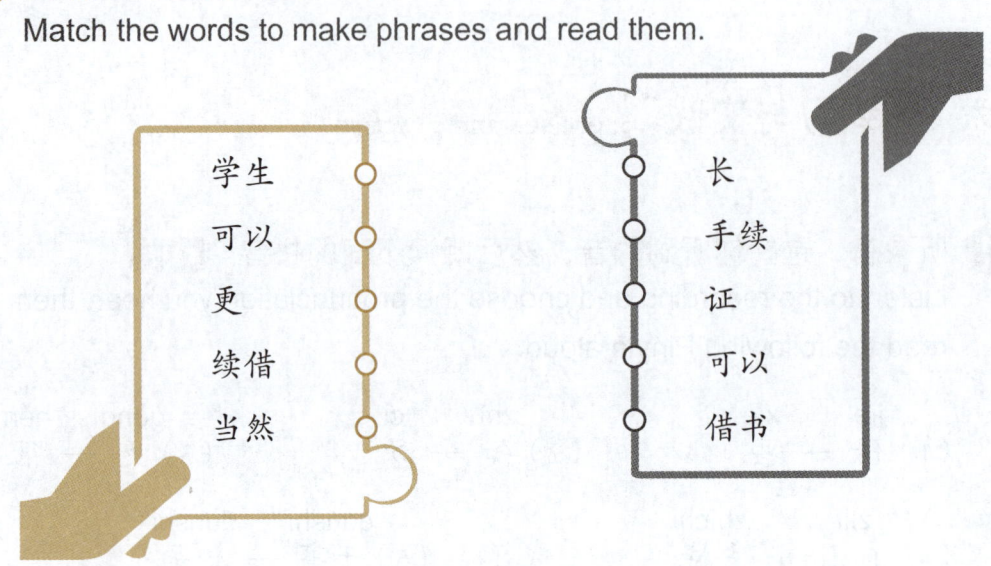

3 连线组成短语，并读一读。
Match the words to make phrases and read them.

学生	长
可以	手续
更	证
续借	可以
当然	借书

4 替换练习：先替换画线的部分，然后和同学一起模仿对话。
Substitution drills: Replace the underlined parts first, then imitate the following dialogue with your classmates.

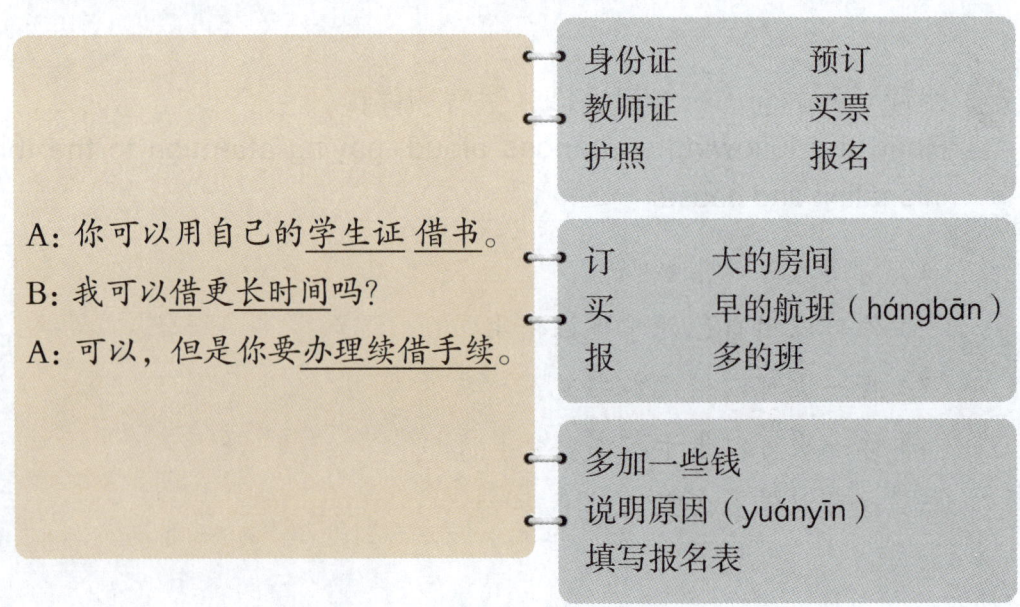

A：你可以用自己的<u>学生证</u> <u>借书</u>。
B：我可以借<u>更长</u>时间吗？
A：可以，但是你要<u>办理续借手续</u>。

身份证	预订
教师证	买票
护照	报名

订	大的房间
买	早的航班（hángbān）
报	多的班

多加一些钱
说明原因（yuányīn）
填写报名表

5 完成对话，并和同学一起表演对话的内容。
Complete the following dialogues, then act them out with your classmates.

（1）A：请问可以提前预订机票吗？

B：可以。你可以_____自己的护照预订。

A：最长可以提前_____长时间呢？

B：你可以提前半年预订。

A：我可以提前_____长时间吗？

B：可以，_____预订以后不能退（tuì）。

（2）A：请帮我_____一下儿入住_____。

B：好的，_____需要_____您的身份证办理。

A：有哪几种房间呢？

B：我们有单人间，也有双人间。

A：有_____好一点儿的房间吗？

B：有，我们还有海景（hǎijǐng）房等多种房间。

6 看视频，先回答问题，然后和同学一起表演视频的内容。
Watch the video and answer the questions. Then act out the video with your classmates.

（1）男的想做什么？

（2）女的是怎么回答他的？

> 视频：8.1 可以借更长时间吗？

7 用下面的词语介绍一下儿自己去图书馆借书的经历。
Talk about your experience of borrowing books from the library with the following words.

用　借　次　更　但是　办理　续借　手续

8 汉字练习：看汉字笔画笔顺动态图，并跟着书写。
Practice Chinese characters: Look at the animated illustrations of the strokes and the order of strokes of the following characters, and then write them down.

jiè
借

jiǔ
久

dàn
但

xù
续

第八课　汉字笔画笔顺动态图

第九课 Lesson 9

你为什么想来我们公司工作呢
Nǐ wèi shénme xiǎng lái wǒmen gōngsī gōngzuò ne

重点提示

- **交际功能**：工作面试。
- **主要生词**：面试、贵、全球性、申请、岗位、因为、觉得、专业、离开、以前、以前、发展。
- **主要语言点**：为什么，因为，觉得。
- **文化小常识**：中国学生找工作。

一 看图讨论 Look at the picture and discuss

1. 他们在做什么？ What are they doing?
2. 他们可能会说什么？ What might they say?

二 》》 课文 Text

听录音回答问题 Listen to the recording and answer the following questions.

1. 女的问了一些什么问题？ What questions did the woman ask?
2. 男的是怎么回答这些问题的？ How did the man answer these questions?

Nǐ wèi shénme xiǎng lái wǒmen gōngsī gōngzuò ne
你为什么想来我们公司工作呢 9-1

nǚ: Nǐ hǎo! Huānyíng nǐ cānjiā wǒmen gōngsī de miànshì.
女：你好！欢迎你参加我们公司的面试。

nán: Xièxie!
男：谢谢！

nǚ: Nǐ wèi shénme xiǎng lái wǒmen gōngsī gōngzuò ne?
女：你为什么想来我们公司工作呢？

nán: Yīnwèi guì gōngsī shì quánqiúxìng de dà gōngsī.
男：因为贵公司是全球性的大公司。

nǚ: Nǐ wèi shénme shēnqǐng zhège gǎngwèi?
女：你为什么申请这个岗位？

nán: Yīnwèi wǒ juéde wǒ de zhuānyè shìhé zhège gǎngwèi.
男：因为我觉得我的专业适合这个岗位。

nǚ: Nǐ wèi shénme líkāi yǐqián de gōngsī?
女：你为什么离开以前的公司？

nán: Yīnwèi wǒ xiǎng dào gèng dà de gōngsī gōngzuò, yǒu gèng hǎo de
男：因为我想到更大的公司工作，有更好的

fāzhǎn.
发展。

三 〉 生词 New words 9-2

1. 为什么		wèi shénme		why
2. 面试	动词	miànshì		interview
3. 贵	形容词	guì		(honorific) your
4. 全球性	名词	quánqiúxìng		global
全球	名词	quánqiú		the whole world
5. 申请	动词	shēnqǐng		apply
6. 岗位	名词	gǎngwèi		post, job
7. 因为	连词	yīnwèi		because
8. 觉得	动词	juéde		feel, think
9. 专业	名词	zhuānyè		major
10. 离开	动词	líkāi		leave
11. 以前	名词	yǐqián		former time
12. 发展	名词	fāzhǎn		development

四 主要语言点 Main language points

1 你为什么想来我们公司工作呢?

"为什么"用来询问原因或目的,放在句首、句中、句尾都可以。例如:
"为什么" is used to inquire the reason or purpose, and can be used at the beginning, middle, or end of a sentence. For example:

(1) 为什么没有人来呢?
(2) 你们为什么想参加这个培训班?
(3) 这是为什么?
(4) 他今天为什么迟到?

▶ 视频:9.1 你为什么想来我们公司工作呢? (1)

2 因为贵公司是全球性的大公司。

"因为……所以……"连接因果复句,表达事情的原因和结果。其中,"因为"和"所以"都可以单独使用,"因为"表示原因,"所以"表示结果。例如:

"因为……所以……" connects a cause-effect compound sentence, expressing the cause and effect of something. Among them, both "因为" and "所以" can be used independently. "因为" indicates the cause, and "所以" indicates the effect. For example:

(1) 我不喜欢吃肉,因为怕长胖(pàng)。
(2) 我今天起晚了,所以迟到了。

（3）A：你为什么学汉语？

　　　B：因为我想了解中国的文化，所以学汉语。

（4）A：马文今天为什么没有来？

　　　B：因为他病了，所以没有来。

▶ 视频：9.1 你为什么想来我们公司工作呢？（1）

3 因为我觉得我的专业适合这个岗位。

"觉得"是一个动词，表示某人对他人或某种情况的主观看法、意见或态度，相当于"认为"，但是语气比较轻。例如：

"觉得" is a verb showing someone's subjective view, opinion or attitude towards others or a certain situation, which is equivalent to "认为", but the tone is more moderate. For example:

（1）同学们觉得李老师的课上得非常好。

（2）我觉得自己这次考得不好。

（3）我觉得这个办法很有用。

▶ 视频：9.2 因为我觉得我的专业适合这个岗位。

五 文化小常识 General knowledge of culture

中国学生找工作

现在，中国每年都有上千万的毕业生找工作，包括从国外留学回国的学生。各类用人单位在招聘毕业生时，除了看应聘者的毕业证书和其他各类能力证书等基本资料外，都有面试这个环节。面试成绩的好坏成为毕业生找工作成败的决定性因素。其中，应聘者的口头表达能力和语言交际能力又是影响他们面试成绩的重要因素。

Chinese Students Looking for Jobs

Nowadays, there are tens of millions of graduates in China looking for jobs every year, including returned overseas students. When employers recruit graduates, in addition to consulting applicants' graduation certificates, various competence certificates, and other basic information, they also conduct interviews. Interview results have become a decisive factor for graduates to get job offers and candidates' oral expression abilities and language communication skills are essential factors that affect their interview results.

六 练习与实践 Exercises and practice

1 听录音，选择你听到的音，然后朗读下面的拼音。 9-3
Listen to the recording and choose the pronunciation you hear, then read the following Pinyin aloud.

（1）岗位 — 敢为
　　gǎngwèi　gǎn wéi

（2）盛情 — 申请
　　shèngqíng　shēnqǐng

（3）学的 — 觉得
　　xué de　juéde

（4）适合 — 十个
　　shìhé　shí gè

　　　　líkāi　　　lìhai　　　　　　　　　　jǐ jiàn　　yǐqián
（5）离开 — 厉害　　　　　　（6）几件 — 以前

　　　　zhuānyè　chuányuè　　　　　　 miànshì　miǎnshì
（7）专业 — 传阅　　　　　　（8）面试 — 免试

2 朗读下面的句子，注意语调、停顿和重音。
Read the following sentences aloud, paying attention to the intonation, pause and stress.

（1）你为什么想来我们公司工作呢？
（2）因为贵公司是全球性的大公司。
（3）你为什么申请这个岗位？
（4）因为我觉得我的专业适合这个岗位。
（5）你为什么离开以前的公司？
（6）因为我想到更大的公司工作，有更好的发展。

3 连线组成短语，并读一读。
Match the words to make phrases and read them.

参加　　　　　　　　　学校
申请　　　　　　　　　工作
工作　　　　　　　　　面试
找　　　　　　　　　　岗位
离开　　　　　　　　　表

4 替换练习：先替换画线的部分，然后和同学一起模仿对话。
Substitution drills: Replace the underlined parts first, then imitate the following dialogues with your classmates.

（1）A：你为什么想来<u>我们公司工作</u>？

　　　B：因为<u>贵公司是全球性的大公司</u>。

来中国留学	我对中国文化很感兴趣（xìngqù）
学习汉语	学好汉语可以更好地了解（liǎojiě）中国
练习太极拳	练习太极拳可以健身

（2）A：你为什么<u>申请这个岗位</u>呢？

　　　B：因为我觉得<u>自己比较适合这个岗位</u>。

对中国文化感兴趣	中国文化很有意思
想了解中国	中国的发展非常快
想健身	健身的好处非常多

5 连词成句。
Arrange the words to make sentences.

（1）为什么　留学　你　去　想　中国　呢

_____？

（2）公司　因为　的　全球性　这个　很　有名

_____。

（3）有　汉语　我　很　意思　学　觉得

_____。

（4）为什么　这个　申请　你　专业

_____？

（5）适合　我　当　自己　觉得　老师

_____。

6 用下面的词语介绍一下儿你将来的工作计划及其原因。
Introduce your future work plan and explain the reasons with the following words.

因为　全球性　公司　岗位　觉得　专业　适合

7 看视频，先回答问题，然后和同学一起表演视频的内容。
Watch the video and answer the questions. Then act out the video with your classmates.

（1）女的问了哪几个问题？

（2）男的是怎么回答这些问题的？

▶ 视频：9.3 你为什么想来我们公司工作呢？（2）

8 四人一组，一人扮演求职者，三人扮演招聘者，模拟进行面试对话。
Work in groups of four. One person plays an applicant, and the other three play recruiters to simulate a dialogue in an interview.

实用交际汉语 3
Practical Communicative Chinese

9 汉字练习：看汉字笔画笔顺动态图，并跟着书写。
Practice Chinese characters: Look at the animated illustrations of the strokes and the order of strokes of the following characters, and then write them down.

wèi
为

quán
全

shēn
申

gǎng
岗

yīn
因

jué
觉

zhuān
专

第九课 你为什么想来我们公司工作呢

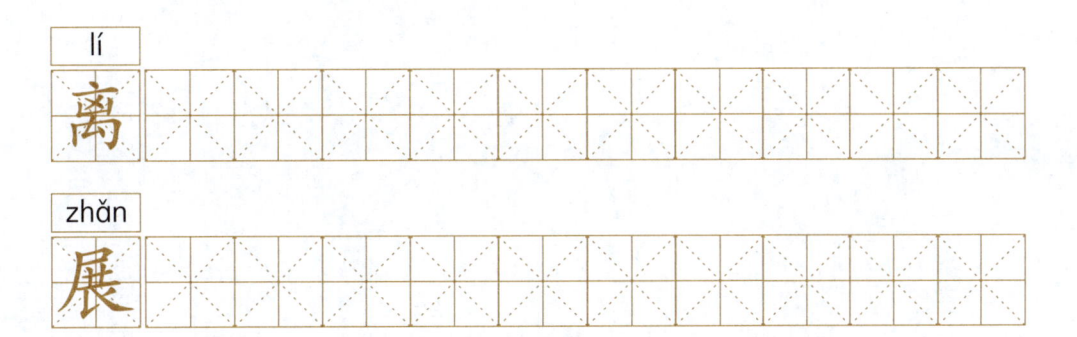

lí
离

zhǎn
展

第九课 汉字笔画笔顺动态图

综合实践一

Lesson 10 第十课

Wǒ xiǎng shēnqǐng Zhōngguó Zhèngfǔ Jiǎngxuéjīn
我想申请中国政府奖学金

重点提示

- 交际功能：咨询奖学金申请的注意事项。
- 主要生词：政府、奖学金、提交、材料、学历、证书、交、驻、大使馆。
- 主要语言点：至，句式"除了……之外，还/也……"。
- 文化小常识：中国政府奖学金。

一 看图讨论 Look at the picture and discuss

1. 图中的小孩儿拿的是什么？ What is the child holding in the picture?
2. 你知道怎么申请吗？ Do you know how to apply?

二 课文 Text

听录音回答问题 Listen to the recording and answer the following questions.

1. 他们在谈论什么？ What are they talking about?
2. 马文问了一些什么问题？ What questions did Ma Wen ask?
3. 王老师是怎么回答这些问题的？ How did Ms. Wang answer these questions?

Wǒ xiǎng shēnqǐng Zhōngguó Zhèngfǔ Jiǎngxuéjīn
我 想 申请 中国 政府 奖学金 10-1

Mǎ Wén: Wáng lǎoshī, wǒ xiǎng shēnqǐng Zhōngguó Zhèngfǔ Jiǎngxuéjīn.
马 文： 王 老师，我 想 申请 中国 政府 奖学金。

Wáng lǎoshī: Hěn hǎo! Wǒ zhīchí nǐ.
王 老师： 很 好！我 支持 你。

Mǎ Wén: Nín zhīdào shēnqǐng de shíjiān ma?
马 文： 您 知道 申请 的 时间 吗？

Wáng lǎoshī: Yìbān shì měi nián de yī yuè zhì sì yuè.
王 老师： 一般 是 每 年 的 一月 至 四月。

Mǎ Wén: Shēnqǐng de shíhou xūyào tíjiāo nǎxiē cáiliào ne?
马 文： 申请 的 时候 需要 提交 哪些 材料 呢？

Wáng lǎoshī: Chúle shēnqǐngbiǎo zhīwài, hái yào tíjiāo xuélì zhèngshū děng
王 老师： 除了 申请表 之外，还要 提交 学历 证书 等

cáiliào.
材料。

101

Mǎ Wén:			Zhèxiē cáiliào jiāo gěi shéi ne?	
马 文:			这些材料交给谁呢?	
Wáng lǎoshī:			Shēnqǐng cáiliào kěyǐ jiāo gěi Zhōngguó zhù Tàiguó dàshǐguǎn.	
王 老师:			申请材料可以交给中国驻泰国大使馆。	
Mǎ Wén:			Xièxie Wáng lǎoshī de jièshào!	
马 文:			谢谢王老师的介绍!	
Wáng lǎoshī:			Bú kèqi!	
王 老师:			不客气!	

三 生词 New words 🔊 10-2

1.	中国政府奖学金	专有名词	Zhōngguó Zhèngfǔ Jiǎngxuéjīn	Chinese government scholarship
	政府	名词	zhèngfǔ	government
	奖学金	名词	jiǎngxuéjīn	scholarship
2.	支持	动词	zhīchí	support
3.	一般	形容词	yìbān	general
4.	至	动词	zhì	to
5.	提交	动词	tíjiāo	submit
6.	材料	名词	cáiliào	material
7.	除了……之外		chúle……zhīwài	besides
8.	申请表	名词	shēnqǐngbiǎo	application form
9.	还	副词	hái	also
10.	学历	名词	xuélì	education background

11. 证书	名词	zhèngshū	certificate
12. 交	动词	jiāo	submit
13. 驻	动词	zhù	be stationed
14. 大使馆	名词	dàshǐguǎn	embassy

四 主要语言点 Main language points

1 一般是每年的一月至四月。

这句中的"至"是一个动词,表示"到"的意思,可以用来连接两个时间点或两个地点,也可以用来连接两个时间段,还可以用来连接具有一定顺序的两个事物。注意,"至"前后的时间要符合从短到长或从早到晚的逻辑顺序。例如:

In this sentence, "至" is a verb, which means "to" and can be used to connect two points of time or two places. It can also be used to connect two periods of time or two things in a certain order. Note that the time before and after "至" should conform to logical order, such as from short to long, or from early to late, etc. For example:

(1) 我们上午上课的时间是八点至十二点。(连接时间点)
(2) 这是北京至广州的列车(lièchē)时刻表。(连接地点)
(3) 他每个月休息三至四天。(连接时间段)
(4) 中文水平考试中,一至三级属于(shǔyú)初级。
　　(连接等级水平)

▶ 视频:10.1 一般是每年的一月至四月。

2 除了申请表之外，还要提交学历证书等材料。

汉语中，"除了……之外，还 / 也……"表示排除一部分，补充其他的。句子的主语放在句首，或者放在"还 / 也"的前边。例如：

In Chinese, "除了……之外, 还 / 也……" indicates that there are still others besides the part being mentioned. The subject is put at the beginning of the sentence or before "还 / 也". For example:

（1）我们在中国除了学习汉语之外，还了解了很多中国文化。
（2）她除了会唱中文歌之外，还会画中国画。
（3）除了去过北京之外，她也去过香港和澳门（Àomén）。
（4）除了会踢足球之外，马文也会打篮球。

视频：10.2 申请的时候需要提交哪些材料呢？

五 文化小常识 General knowledge of culture

中国政府奖学金

中国政府奖学金由中国教育部主管，中国国家留学基金管理委员会具体负责办理。中国政府奖学金设立的目的是增进中国人民与世界各国人民的相互了解和友谊，发展中国与世界各国在教育、科技、文化、经贸等领域的交流与合作。可供申请的学习项目包括本科生、硕士研究生、博士研究生、汉语进修生、普通进修生、高级进修生等。申请成功后的奖学金费用包括学费、住宿费、生活费、基本教材费、紧急医疗费、一次性安置费和一次性城市间交通费等。

Chinese Government Scholarship

Chinese government scholarship, managed by Chinese Ministry of Education and taken care of by China Scholarship Council, aims to enhance mutual understanding and friendship between Chinese people and people from all over the world, and to develop exchanges and cooperation between China and countries around the world in education, technology, culture, economy, trade and other fields. The study programmes available for application include those for Bachelor degree, Master's degree, doctoral degree, further study of Chinese, general further study and advanced further study. The scholarship includes tuition, accommodation fees, living expenses, fees for basic teaching materials, emergency medical expenses, one-time resettlement fees, and one-time inter-city transportation fees, etc.

六 练习与实践 Exercises and practice

1 听录音，选择你听到的音，然后朗读下面的拼音。 10-3
Listen to the recording and choose the pronunciation you hear, then read the following Pinyin aloud.

（1）表 — 漂　　biǎo — piāo
（2）驻 — 主　　zhù — zhǔ
（3）至 — 只　　zhì — zhǐ
（4）一般 — 几盘　　yìbān — jǐ pán
（5）尺子 — 支持　　chǐzi — zhīchí
（6）低效 — 提交　　dīxiào — tíjiāo
（7）材料 — 再要　　cáiliào — zài yào

105

(8) 学习 — 学历　　　　(9) 证书 — 胜出
　　xuéxí　　xuélì　　　　　zhèngshū　shèngchū

(10) 下决心 — 奖学金　　(11) 大使馆 — 他付款
　　xià juéxīn　jiǎngxuéjīn　　dàshǐguǎn　tā fùkuǎn

2 朗读下面的句子，注意语调、语气和停顿。
Read the following sentences aloud, paying attention to the intonation, tone and pause.

（1）我想申请中国政府奖学金。
（2）您知道申请的时间吗？
（3）一般是每年的一月至四月。
（4）申请的时候需要提交哪些材料呢？
（5）除了申请表之外，还要提交学历证书等材料。
（6）这些材料交给谁呢？
（7）申请材料可以交给中国驻泰国大使馆。

3 连线组成短语，并读一读。
Match the words to make phrases and read them.

申请　　　　　　　　证书
提前　　　　　　　　材料
学历　　　　　　　　时间
提交　　　　　　　　预订

4 完成下面的对话，然后和同学一起表演对话的内容。
Complete the following dialogue, then act it out with your classmates.

A：昨天你去中国_____泰国大使馆做什么？

B：我去_____中国政府奖学金的_____材料。

A：主要_____哪些材料呢？

B：_____申请表_____，_____ _____了本科毕业证、HSK 等级证书等。

A：你知道中国政府奖学金的_____时间吗？

B：_____是每年的一月_____四月。

5 替换练习。
Substitution drills.

（1）奖学金的申请时间一般是九月至十月。

图书馆的开放	上午九点	下午五点
考试的报名	每年三月	五月
国庆放假	十月一号	七号

（2）除了申请表之外，还要提交学历证明等材料。

北京	去了上海、广州	城市
泰国	有越南、马来西亚	国家
苹果	买了梨、西瓜	水果

107

（3）申请材料可以交给<u>中国驻泰国大使馆</u>。	中国　　　马来西亚 越南　　　中国 新加坡　　中国

❻ 看视频，先回答问题，然后和同学一起表演视频的内容。
Watch the video and answer the questions. Then act out the video with your classmates.

（1）中国政府奖学金的申请时间是什么时候？
（2）申请中国政府奖学金需要提交哪些材料？

▷ 视频：10.3 您知道申请的时间吗？

❼ 用下面的词语介绍一下儿自己申请中国各类奖学金的经过。
Introduce the process that you apply for various Chinese scholarships with the following words.

申请　奖学金　提交　材料　至　证书　学历
除了……之外　还　一般

❽ 汉字练习：看汉字笔画笔顺动态图，并跟着书写。
Practice Chinese characters: Look at the animated illustrations of the strokes and the order of strokes of the following characters, and then write them down.

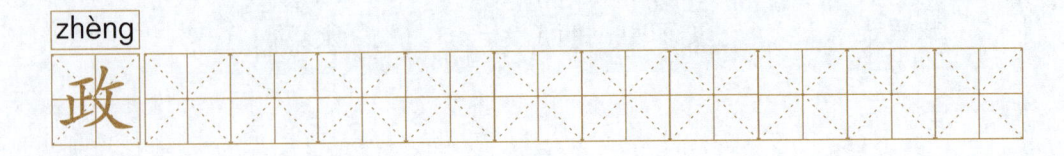

zhèng
政

第十课 我想申请中国政府奖学金

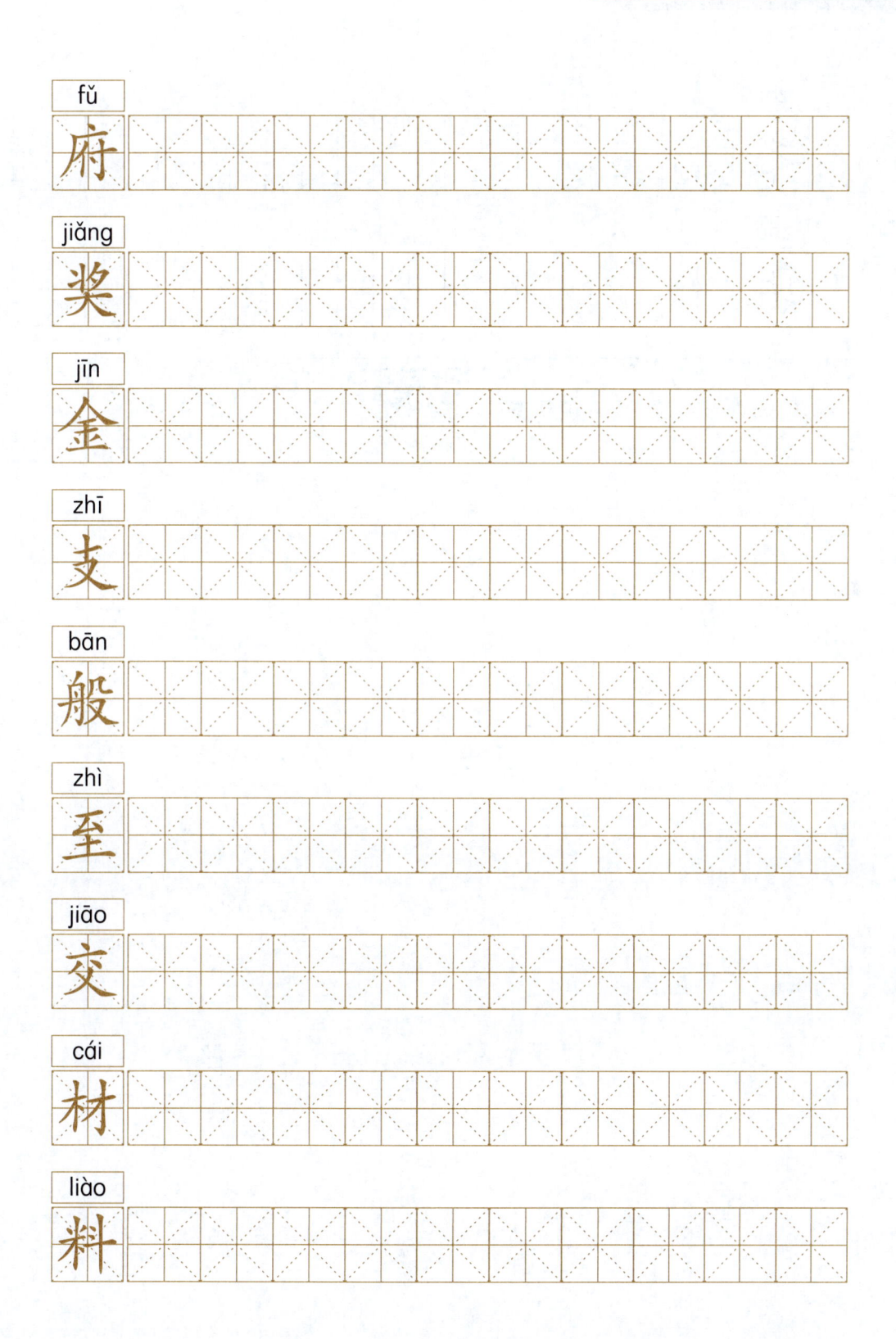

fǔ
府

jiǎng
奖

jīn
金

zhī
支

bān
般

zhì
至

jiāo
交

cái
材

liào
料

zhī
之

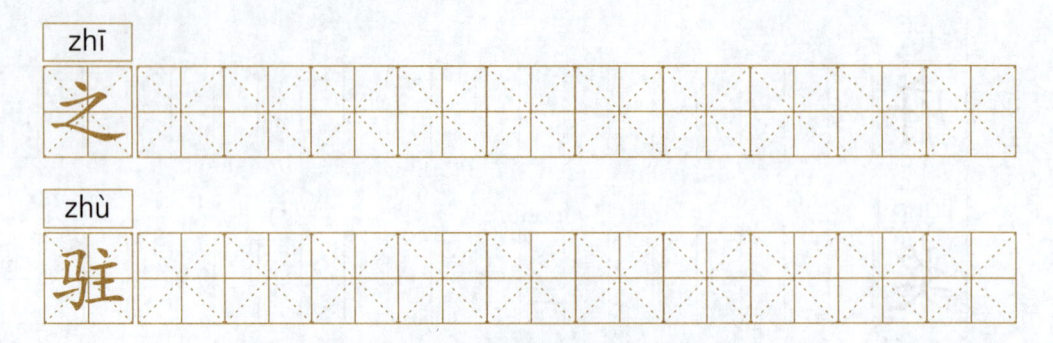

zhù
驻

第十课　汉字笔画笔顺动态图

Lesson 11 第十一课

Wǒ xiǎng bànlǐ liúxué qiānzhèng
我想办理留学签证

重点提示

- 交际功能：办理留学签证。
- 主要生词：签证、交往、资助、毕业、当。
- 主要语言点：越来越……，代词"它"。
- 文化小常识：中国留学签证。

一 看图讨论 Look at the picture and discuss

1. 他们在做什么？ What are they doing?
2. 他们可能说什么？ What might they say?

111

二 》 课 文 Text

听录音回答问题 Listen to the recording and answer the following questions.

1. 马文在做什么？ What is Ma Wen doing?
2. 签证官问了一些什么问题？ What questions did the visa officer ask?
3. 马文是怎么回答这些问题的？ How did Ma Wen answer these questions?

Wǒ xiǎng bànlǐ liúxué qiānzhèng
我 想 办理 留学 签证 🔊 11-1

qiānzhèngguān: Nǐ hǎo! Qǐngwèn nǐ xiǎng bànlǐ shénme yèwù?
签证官： 你好！请问 你 想 办理 什么 业务？

Mǎ Wén: Wǒ xiǎng bànlǐ liúxué qiānzhèng.
马 文： 我 想 办理 留学 签证。

qiānzhèngguān: Qǐngwèn nǐ jiào shénme míngzi?
签证官： 请问 你叫 什么 名字？

Mǎ Wén: Wǒ jiào Mǎ Wén.
马 文： 我叫 马 文。

qiānzhèngguān: Nǐ wèi shénme xiǎng qù Zhōngguó liúxué?
签证官： 你为 什么 想 去 中国 留学？

Mǎ Wén: Yīnwèi Zhōngguó xiànzài fāzhǎn hěn hǎo, hé wǒmen guójiā
马 文： 因为 中国 现在 发展 很 好，和我们 国家

de jiāowǎng yě yuè lái yuè duō.
的 交往 也 越 来 越 多。

qiānzhèngguān： Nǐ shēnqǐngle nǎ suǒ dàxué? Wèi shénme xiǎng qù zhè suǒ
签证官： 你 申请了 哪 所 大学？为 什么 想 去 这 所

xuéxiào?
学校？

Mǎ Wén： Wǒ shēnqǐngle Jìnán Dàxué, zhè shì yì suǒ hěn hǎo de
马 文： 我 申请了 暨南 大学，这 是 一 所 很 好 的

dàxué, tā de Hànyǔ jiàoxué zhìliàng hěn hǎo.
大学，它 的 汉语 教学 质量 很 好。

qiānzhèngguān： Shéi zīzhù nǐ qù Zhōngguó liúxué?
签证官： 谁 资助 你 去 中国 留学？

Mǎ Wén： Wǒ shēnqǐng dào le Zhōngguó Zhèngfǔ Jiǎngxuéjīn.
马 文： 我 申请 到 了 中国 政府 奖学金。

qiānzhèngguān： Nǐ yǐhòu yǒu shénme dǎsuàn?
签证官： 你 以后 有 什么 打算？

Mǎ Wén： Wǒ dǎsuàn bìyè yǐhòu huí guó dāng Hànyǔ lǎoshī.
马 文： 我 打算 毕业 以后 回国 当 汉语 老师。

三 》 生 词 New words 11-2

1. 签证	名词	qiānzhèng	visa
2. 签证官	名词	qiānzhèngguān	visa officer
3. 交往	动词	jiāowǎng	associate, contact
4. 越来越		yuè lái yuè	more and more

5. 它	代词	tā	it
6. 资助	动词	zīzhù	subsidise
7. 毕业	动词	bìyè	graduate
8. 当	动词	dāng	work as

四 主要语言点 Main language points

1 因为中国现在发展很好，和我们国家的交往也越来越多。

"越来越"表示随着时间的推移，程度上发生的变化，后边常加上形容词或心理动词，构成"越来越 + 形容词 / 心理动词"结构。例如：

"越来越" indicates the change in degree as time passes by. It is often followed by an adjective or a psychological verb to form the structure "越来越 + adjective/psychological verb". For example:

（1）他的汉语成绩（chéngjì）越来越好。
（2）这里的人越来越多。
（3）风越来越大。
（4）我越来越喜欢中国文化了。

注意：形容词或心理动词的前边不能再加程度副词。例如：

Note: An adverb of degree cannot be put before an adjective or a psychological verb. For example:

（5）*雨越来越很大。
（6）*生词越来越非常多。

（7）*我越来越非常喜欢汉语。

> 视频：11.1 中国和我们国家的交往也越来越多。

② 它的汉语教学质量很好。

"它"是一个代词，指代人以外的事物。一般用于单数事物，"它"的复数是"它们"。比如：

"它" is a pronoun, referring to things other than people. It is usually used for singular things, and the plural form of "它" is "它们". For example:

（1）这种苹果很好吃，它也很便宜。
（2）这个词大家要记好，以后会经常用它。
（3）网上学习很方便，我们现在都用它。

> 视频：11.2 它的汉语教学质量很好。

五 文化小常识 General knowledge of culture

中国留学签证

中国留学签证的一般申请办法与流程是：申请者先通过相关大学的网站进行在线申请，提交所需申请信息，并打印出系统自动生成的申请表。申请者本人在申请表上签名后，连同其他申请材料一起提交给相关大学。通过考试或面试被录取后，该大学会给申请者发送"录取通知书"等材料。被录取者再持上面的材料及护照等前往中国驻申请人国家的使领馆办理入境学习签证。

China Student Visa

The method and process for applying a China student visa are as follows: The candidate first applies on the website of the related university, submits the application information required, and prints the application form automatically generated by the system. After signing the application form, the applicant submits it along with other application materials to the university. After the applicant passes the exams and interviews, the university will send him/her materials such as a "Letter of Admission". The applicant who has been admitted should then go to the Chinese embassy or consulate in the applicant's country with the above materials and his/her passport to apply for a student visa.

六 练习与实践 Exercises and practice

1 听录音，选择你听到的音，然后朗读下面的拼音。 11-3
Listen to the recording and choose the pronunciation you hear, then read the following Pinyin aloud.

(1) 牛 niú — 留 liú　　(2) 当 dāng — 汤 tāng　　(3) 之 zhī — 资 zī

(4) 办理 bànlǐ — 帮你 bāng nǐ　　(5) 六届 liù jiè — 留学 liúxué

（6）见证 — 签证
　　jiànzhèng　qiānzhèng

（7）发展 — 花展
　　fāzhǎn　huāzhǎn

（8）教学 — 小学
　　jiàoxué　xiǎoxué

（9）有酒 — 优秀
　　yǒu jiǔ　yōuxiù

（10）吃醋 — 资助
　　chīcù　zīzhù

（11）毕业 — 皮鞋
　　bìyè　píxié

2 朗读下面的句子，注意语调、语气和停顿。
Read the following sentences aloud, paying attention to the intonation, tone and pause.

（1）你为什么想去中国留学？
（2）因为中国现在发展很好，和我们国家的交往也越来越多。
（3）你申请了哪所大学？
（4）这是一所很好的大学。
（5）谁资助你去中国留学？
（6）我申请到了中国政府奖学金。
（7）你以后有什么打算？
（8）我打算毕业以后回国当汉语老师。

3 连线组成短语，并读一读。
Match the words to make phrases and read them.

办理	资助
发展	以后
政府	签证
毕业	教学
汉语	很快

❹ 替换练习。
Substitution drills.

(1) 中国的发展越来越好。

这几天的天气	热
这几课的生词	多
他的身体	健康

(2) 我打算毕业以后回国当汉语老师。

她打算考完试	去旅游
小王打算做完作业	看电视
公司要求大家十一点	去吃饭

(3) 谁资助你去中国留学？

教	学汉语
帮	买票
送	去机场

❺ 完成下面的对话，然后和同学一起表演对话的内容。
Complete the following dialogue, then act it out with your classmates.

A：昨天你去中国_____泰国大使馆做什么？

B：我去_____中国留学_____。

A：你_____去中国留学呢？

B：_____中国现在_____很好，我们国家和中国的交往也_____多。

❻ 看视频，先回答问题，然后和同学一起表演视频的内容。
Watch the video and answer the questions. Then act out the video with your classmates.

(1) 马文为什么想去中国留学？

（2）他申请了哪所大学？为什么申请那所大学？

▷ 视频：11.3 你为什么想去中国留学？

7 用下面的词语介绍一下儿自己或者朋友办理留学签证的过程。
Introduce the process that you or your friend apply for the student visa with the following words.

办理　留学　签证　发展　资助　交往　优秀

8 汉字练习：看汉字笔画笔顺动态图，并跟着书写。
Practice Chinese characters: Look at the animated illustrations of the strokes and the order of strokes of the following characters, and then write them down.

qiān
签

guān
官

yuè
越

tā
它

zī
资

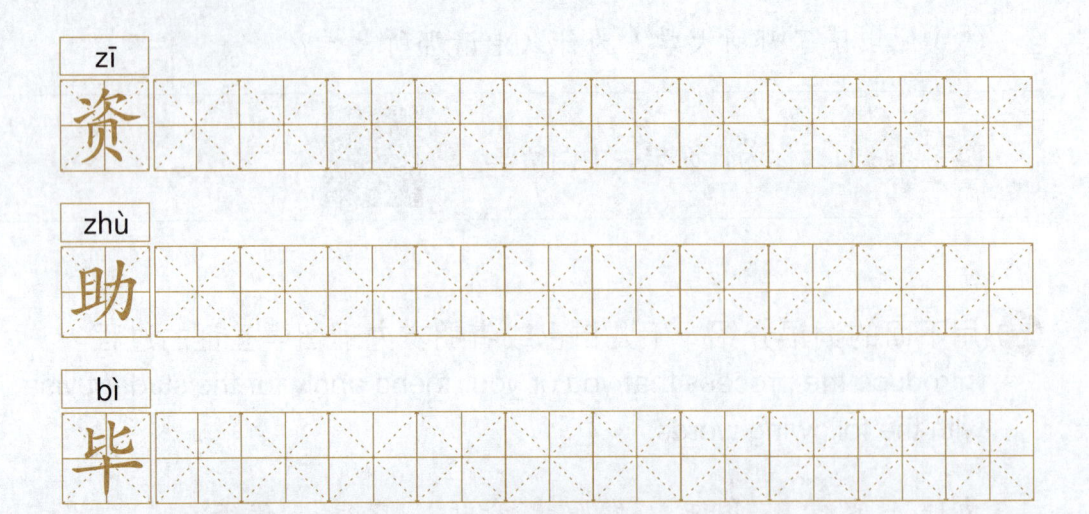

zhù
助

bì
毕

第十一课　汉字笔画笔顺动态图

第十二课 Lesson 12

Wǒ xiǎng zīxún yíxiàr Guǎngjiāohuì de shì
我想咨询一下儿广交会的事

重点提示

- **交际功能**：咨询广交会。
- **主要生词**：咨询、举办、中旬、上旬、地点、贸易、合作、交流。
- **主要语言点**：副词"只"，连词"与"。
- **文化小常识**：广交会。

一 看图讨论 Look at the picture and discuss

1. 下图是什么？ What is in the picture below?
2. 你参加过吗？ Have you participated in it?

121

二 课文 Text

听录音回答问题 Listen to the recording and answer the following questions.

1. 马文在做什么？他问了一些什么问题？ What is Ma Wen doing? What questions did he ask?
2. 女的是怎么回答这些问题的？ How did the woman answer these questions?
3. 你知道这是什么会吗？主要是做什么的？ Do you know about this fair? What is its main purpose?

我想咨询一下儿广交会的事
Wǒ xiǎng zīxún yíxiàr Guǎngjiāohuì de shì 🔊 12-1

接线员 jiēxiànyuán： 您好！这里是中国广交会，需要帮忙吗？
Nín hǎo! Zhèlǐ shì Zhōngguó Guǎngjiāohuì, xūyào bāngmáng ma?

马文 Mǎ Wén： 您好！我想咨询一下儿广交会的事。
Nín hǎo! Wǒ xiǎng zīxún yíxiàr Guǎngjiāohuì de shì.

接线员 jiēxiànyuán： 好的，请讲。
Hǎo de, qǐng jiǎng.

马文 Mǎ Wén： 请问广交会一般什么时候举办？
Qǐngwèn Guǎngjiāohuì yìbān shénme shíhou jǔbàn?

接线员 jiēxiànyuán： 每年有两次，春季在四月中旬至五月上旬，秋季在十月中旬至十一月上旬。
Měi nián yǒu liǎng cì, chūnjì zài sì yuè zhōngxún zhì wǔ yuè shàngxún, qiūjì zài shí yuè zhōngxún zhì shíyī yuè shàngxún.

第十二课 ● 我想咨询一下儿广交会的事

Mǎ Wén: Jǔbàn de dìdiǎn zài nǎr?
马 文：举办的地点在哪儿？

jiēxiànyuán: Dìdiǎn zài Zhōngguó de Guǎngdōng Shěng Guǎngzhōu Shì.
接线员：地点在中国的广东省广州市。

Mǎ Wén: Guǎngjiāohuì zhǐ zuò shāngpǐn màoyì ma?
马 文：广交会只做商品贸易吗？

jiēxiànyuán: Bù, chúle zuò shāngpǐn màoyì wài, hái yǒu hěn duō hézuò yǔ
接线员：不，除了做商品贸易外，还有很多合作与

jiāoliú.
交流。

Mǎ Wén: Xièxie nín de jièshào!
马 文：谢谢您的介绍！

jiēxiànyuán: Bú kèqi! Huānyíng nín lái cānhuì!
接线员：不客气！欢迎您来参会！

三 生词 New words 12-2

1. 咨询	动词	zīxún	consult
2. 广交会	专有名词	Guǎngjiāohuì	Canton Fair (China Import and Export Fair)
3. 举办	动词	jǔbàn	conduct, hold
4. 中旬	名词	zhōngxún	the middle ten-day period of a month

123

	旬	名词	xún	period of ten days
5.	上旬	名词	shàngxún	the first ten-day period of a month
6.	地点	名词	dìdiǎn	place
7.	只	副词	zhǐ	only
8.	贸易	名词	màoyì	trade
9.	合作	动词	hézuò	cooperate
10.	与	连词	yǔ	and
11.	交流	动词	jiāoliú	communicate

四 主要语言点 Main language points

1 广交会只做商品贸易吗?

这句中的"只"是一个表示范围的副词,用来限定与动作有关的事物,意思是除了提到的之外再没有别的。例如:

"只" in this sentence is an adverb indicating scope, which is used to limit something related to an action. It means that there is nothing else except what is mentioned. For example:

(1) 这家书店只卖中文书。(限定动作"卖"的书是"中文书")
(2) 我早餐只吃面包。(限定动作"吃"的东西是"面包")

"只"也可以用来限定与动作有关的事物的数量。例如:

"只" can also be used to limit the number of something related to an action. For example:

（3）我只学了一年太极拳。（限定"学"的时间是"一年"）
（4）我们班只有三个美国学生。（限定"有"的数量是"三个"）

▶ 视频：12.1 广交会只做商品贸易吗？

2 广交会除了做商品贸易外，还有很多合作与交流。

这句中的"与"是一个连词，用来连接两个并列的词或短语。一般来说，这两个词或短语的结构、性质相同，并且在句子中所做的成分也相同。"与"的意思跟连词"和"相近，但常用于正式的交际场合中，用来讨论比较严肃的话题。例如：

"与" in this sentence is a conjunction used to connect two parallel words or phrases. These two words or phrases usually have the same structure and part of speech, and act as the same element in the sentence. The meaning of "与" is similar to that of the conjunction "和", but it is often used on formal communication occasions to discuss more serious topics. For example:

（1）大家应该知道学习与生活的关系。
（2）我最尊敬（zūnjìng）的两个人是父亲与母亲。
（3）教学中，老师与学生之间的关系非常重要。
（4）提高听与说的能力是提高交际水平的重要方法。

▶ 视频：12.1 广交会只做商品贸易吗？

五 文化小常识 General knowledge of culture

广交会

广交会的全名是中国进出口商品交易会，因为在广州举办，所以简称为"广交会"。广交会创办于1957年，每年春、秋两季举办，是商品种类最全、到会商家最多的国际贸易盛会。现在，除传统的现场线下交易外，广交会还举办了网上交易会。在广交会上，人们不但可以做进出口生意，还可以开展多种形式的经济、技术合作与交流。近几年，每届广交会参会的国家和地区有210多个，境外采购商约20万，境内外参展企业近2.5万家。展出的商品包括电子电气产品、计算机、汽车、服装、食品和药品等多种。

Canton Fair

The full name of Canton Fair is China Import and Export Fair, which is called "Canton Fair" for short because it is held in Guangzhou. Founded in 1957, it is held in spring and autumn every year. It is an international trade event having the most varieties of goods and the largest number of merchants. Nowadays, in addition to providing traditional on-site offline transactions, Canton Fair also holds online trade fairs. In the fair, people can not only do import and export business, but also carry out various forms of economic and technological cooperation and exchange. In recent years, each Canton Fair has more than 210 countries and regions, about 200,000 overseas purchasers, and nearly 25,000 domestic and foreign exhibitors to attend. The commodities on display at Canton Fair include electronical products, computers, automobiles, clothing, food and medicine, etc.

六 练习与实践 Exercises and practice

1 听录音，选择你听到的音，然后朗读下面的拼音。 🔊 12-3
Listen to the recording and choose the pronunciation you hear, then read the following Pinyin aloud.

（1）xún — shùn
　　旬 — 顺

（2）zhǐ — chǐ
　　只 — 尺

（3）jǔ — yǔ
　　举 — 与

（4）màoyì — máoyī
　　贸易 — 毛衣

（5）sān píng — shāngpǐn
　　三 瓶 — 商品

（6）zīxún — cíxìng
　　咨询 — 词性

（7）jǔbàn — qǔxìn
　　举办 — 取信

（8）tíqián — dìdiǎn
　　提前 — 地点

（9）gè suǒ — hézuò
　　各 所 — 合作

（10）jiāoliú — xiàoyǒu
　　交流 — 校友

（11）guāng xiāofèi — Guǎngjiāohuì
　　光 消费 — 广交会

2 朗读下面的句子，注意语调、语气和停顿。
Read the following sentences aloud, paying attention to the intonation, tone and pause.

（1）我想咨询一下儿广交会的事。
（2）广交会一般什么时候举办？
（3）春季在四月中旬至五月上旬。
（4）地点在中国的广东省广州市。
（5）广交会只做商品贸易吗？

127

（6）除了做商品贸易外，还有很多合作与交流。

（7）欢迎您来参会！

3 连线组成短语，并读一读。
Match the words to make phrases and read them.

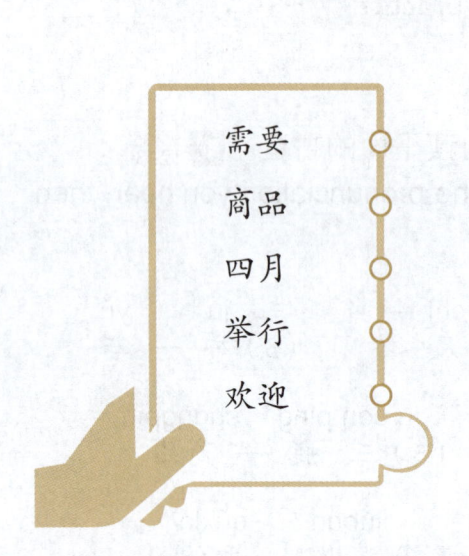

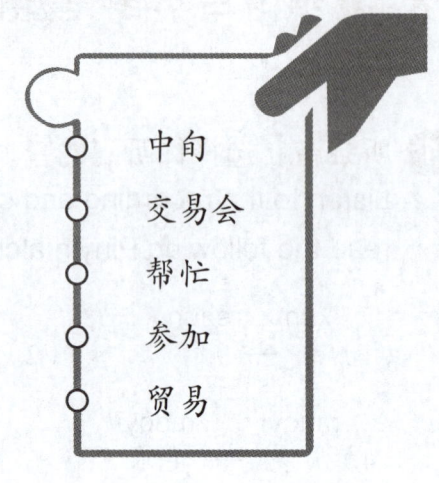

需要　　　　　　　　中旬
商品　　　　　　　　交易会
四月　　　　　　　　帮忙
举行　　　　　　　　参加
欢迎　　　　　　　　贸易

4 替换练习：先替换画线的部分，然后和同学一起模仿对话。
Substitution drills: Replace the underlined parts first, then imitate the following dialogues with your classmates.

（1）A: 广交会只做商品贸易吗？
　　　B: 广交会除了做商品贸易，还有很多合作与交流。

你们	在课堂上学习汉语
王老师	教语法
他们上课	听老师讲

我们	在课堂上学习汉语	有很多参观（cānguān）与考察（kǎochá）
王老师	教语法	教会话（huìhuà）与阅读
他们上课	听老师讲	有讨论与报告（bàogào）

128

（2）欢迎您来参会！ →　大家报名
　　　　　　　　　　　　同学们来听课
　　　　　　　　　　　　各位光临

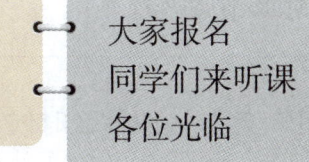

5 完成下面的对话，然后和同学一起表演对话的内容。
Complete the following dialogue, then act it out with your classmates.

A：前几天你去哪儿了？

B：我去_____广交会了。

A：什么是广交会呢？

B：广交会的全名是中国进出口商品交易会，因为在广州_____，所以也叫广交会。

A：广交会_____做商品_____吗？

B：广交会不_____做商品_____，_____有多种技术合作_____交流。

6 用下面的词语介绍一下儿在中国或者你们自己国家举办的大型商品交易会。
Introduce the large-scale commodity trade fair held in China or your own country with the following words.

商品　贸易　举行　中旬　上旬　只　合作　交流　与

7 看视频，先回答问题，然后介绍一下儿你所了解的广交会的情况。
Watch the video and answer the questions. Then introduce what you know about Canton Fair.

（1）广交会一般什么时候举办？

（2）广交会在哪儿举办？

（3）广交会只做商品贸易吗？

▶ 视频：12.2 请问广交会 一般什么时候举办？

8 汉字练习：看汉字笔画笔顺动态图，并跟着书写。
Practice Chinese characters: Look at the animated illustrations of the strokes and the order of strokes of the following characters, and then write them down.

zī
咨

xún
询

jǔ
举

xún
旬

zhǐ
只

yì
易

第十二课 我想咨询一下广交会的事

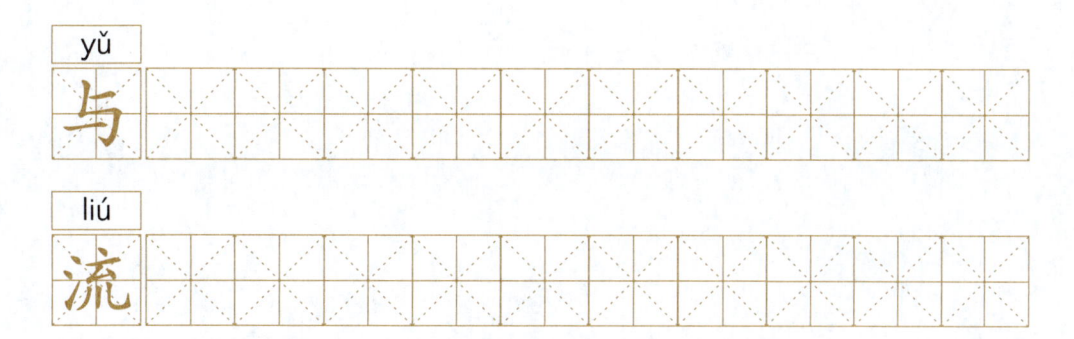

yǔ
与

liú
流

第十二课 汉字笔画笔顺动态图

交际项目四
谈论天气

第十三课 Lesson 13

Jīntiān de tiānqì zěnmeyàng
今天的天气怎么样

重点提示

- 交际功能：谈论天气。
- 主要生词：天气、白天、晴天、多云、雷阵雨、风、级。
- 主要语言点：表示变化的"到"，正反问"A 不 A"。
- 文化小常识：天气预报。

一 看图讨论 Look at the picture and discuss

1. 下图是什么天气？What is the weather like in the picture below?
2. 你喜欢什么天气？What weather do you like?

134

二 课文 Text

听录音回答问题 Listen to the recording and answer the following questions.

1. 马文问了什么？ What did Ma Wen ask?
2. 李安平是怎么回答他的？ How did Li Anping answer him?

Jīntiān de tiānqì zěnmeyàng?
今天的天气怎么样？ 🔊 13-1

Mǎ Wén： Jīntiān de tiānqì zěnmeyàng?
马　文： 今天的天气怎么样？

Lǐ Ānpíng： Báitiān qíngtiān dào duōyún.
李安平： 白天晴天到多云。

Mǎ Wén： Wǎnshang ne?
马　文： 晚上呢？

Lǐ Ānpíng： Wǎnshang yǒu léizhènyǔ.
李安平： 晚上有雷阵雨。

Mǎ Wén： Yǔ dà bu dà?
马　文： 雨大不大？

Lǐ Ānpíng： Bú dà.
李安平： 不大。

Mǎ Wén： Yǒu fēng ma?
马　文： 有风吗？

Lǐ Ānpíng: Yǒu sān dào sì jí dōngnánfēng.
李安平: 有三到四级东南风。

Mǎ Wén: Xièxie nǐ.
马 文: 谢谢你。

Lǐ Ānpíng: Bú kèqi!
李安平: 不客气!

三 》 生 词   New words 13-2

1. 天气	名词	tiānqì	weather
2. 白天	名词	báitiān	daytime
3. 晴天	名词	qíngtiān	fine day
4. 到	动词	dào	to
5. 多云	名词	duōyún	cloudiness
6. 雷阵雨	名词	léizhènyǔ	thundershower
7. 风	名词	fēng	wind
8. 级	名词	jí	force
9. 东南风	名词	dōngnánfēng	southeaster

四 主要语言点 Main language points

1 白天晴天到多云。

这句中的"到"表示某种情况或者状态的发展变化。例如:
"到" in this sentence indicates the development and change of a certain situation or state. For example:

(1) 明天小到中雨。
(2) 晚上中到大雪(xuě)。
(3) 今天有一到三级东南风。

▶ 视频:13.1 今天的天气怎么样?

2 雨大不大?

这个问句是将人或事物正、反两个方面的特点并列起来构成疑问,这样的问句叫正反问。"A(形容词)不A"是这种问句的常见格式之一。例如:

This interrogative sentence is formed by juxtaposing the positive and negative characteristics of people or things. Such interrogative sentences are called affirmative-negative questions. One of the common patterns of this type of questions is "A (adjective) 不 A". For example:

(1) 明天天气冷不冷?
(2) 他的个子高不高?
(3) 学汉语难不难?

137

注意：如果形容词是双音节 AB 形式，正反问的格式为"A 不 AB"。例如：

Note: If the adjective is a two-syllable form of AB, the pattern of the affirmative-negative question is "A 不 AB". For example:

（4）马文的字漂不漂亮？
（5）这里的水果便不便宜？
（6）她昨天生日高不高兴？

▶ 视频：13.2 雨大不大？

五 文化小常识 General knowledge of culture

天气预报

天气预报就是提前一定的时间告诉我们某一地区未来一段时期内的天气情况，如阴、晴、雨、雪、气温、风向、风速等。天气预报在人们的日常生活中具有重要作用。人们的出行、工农业生产和各类大型赛事等都离不开天气预报。现在，我们可以通过广播、电视、网络等多种途径随时了解世界各地的天气情况。

Weather Forecast

Weather forecast is to tell us in advance the weather conditions of a place in a period of time, such as whether it will be cloudy, sunny, rainy, or snowy, and the temperature, wind direction, wind speed and so on. Weather forecast plays an important role in people's daily life. People's travel, industrial and agricultural production and various large-scale events depend on it. At present, we can get to know the weather conditions around the world at any time through radio, television, the Internet and other channels.

六 练习与实践 Exercises and practice

1 听录音，选择你听到的音，然后朗读下面的拼音。 13-3
Listen to the recording and choose the pronunciation you hear, then read the following Pinyin aloud.

(1) 风 fēng — 空 kōng　　(2) 女 nǚ — 雨 yǔ　　(3) 级 jí — 气 qì

(4) 天气 tiānqì — 点击 diǎnjī　　(5) 台前 tái qián — 白天 báitiān

(6) 景点 jǐngdiǎn — 晴天 qíngtiān　　(7) 多云 duōyún — 多人 duō rén

(8) 东南 dōngnán — 天蓝 tiānlán　　(9) 城区 chéngqū — 阵雨 zhènyǔ

2 朗读下面的句子，注意语调、语气和重音。
Read the following sentences aloud, paying attention to the intonation, tone and stress.

(1) 今天的天气怎么样？

(2) 白天晴天到多云。

(3) 晚上呢？

（4）晚上有雷阵雨。

（5）雨大不大？

（6）有风吗？

（7）有三到四级东南风。

3 看图连线。
Look at the pictures and match them with the words.

曼谷 Bangkok	北京 Beijing	广州 Guangzhou	悉尼 Sydney

多云　　晴天　　小雨　　雷阵雨

4 用汉语说出下列图片所示的天气。
Tell the weather conditions in the following pictures in Chinese.

（1）

第十三课　今天的天气怎么样

（2）

（3）

141

❺ 替换练习：先替换画线的部分，然后和同学一起模仿对话。
Substitution drills: Replace the underlined parts first, then imitate the following dialogue with your classmates.

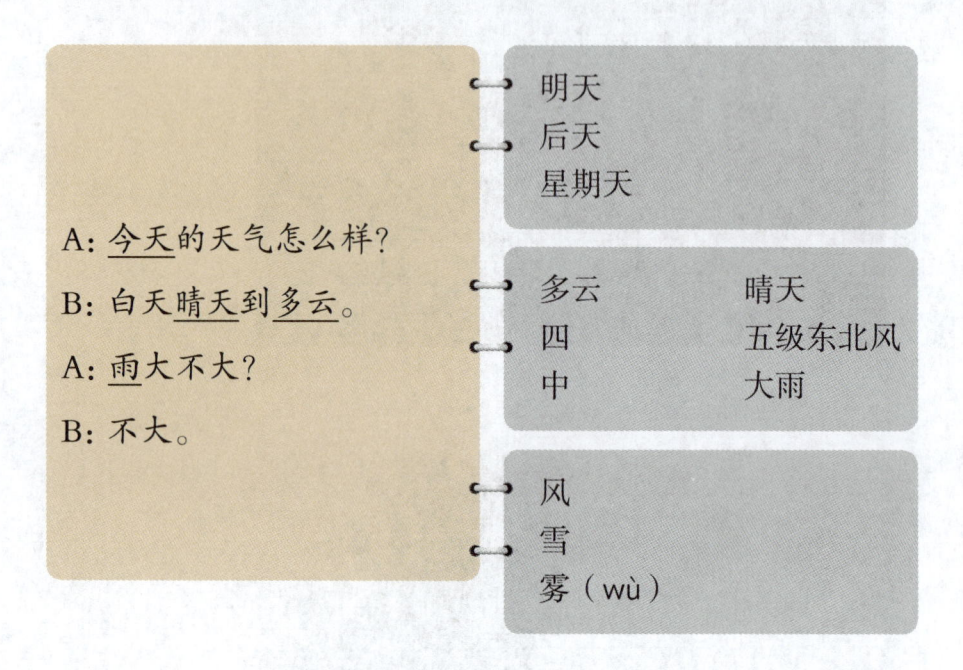

A: 今天的天气怎么样？ B: 白天晴天到多云。 A: 雨大不大？ B: 不大。	明天 后天 星期天 多云　　晴天 四　　　五级东北风 中　　　大雨 风 雪 雾（wù）

❻ 看视频，先回答问题，然后和同学一起表演视频的内容。
Watch the video and answer the questions. Then act out the video with your classmates.

（1）他们在谈论什么？
（2）男的问了什么问题？
（3）女的是怎么回答他的？

▶ 视频：13.1 今天的天气怎么样？

7 上网查询你所在的地区未来一周的天气，并用下面的词语给大家简单预报一下儿。

Surf the Internet and check the weather in your area for the next week, and give a brief forecast to your classmates with the following words.

天气　　白天　　晴天　　多云　　风　　雨　　雷阵雨　　级　　到

8 汉字练习：看汉字笔画笔顺动态图，并跟着书写。

Practice Chinese characters: Look at the animated illustrations of the strokes and the order of strokes of the following characters, and then write them down.

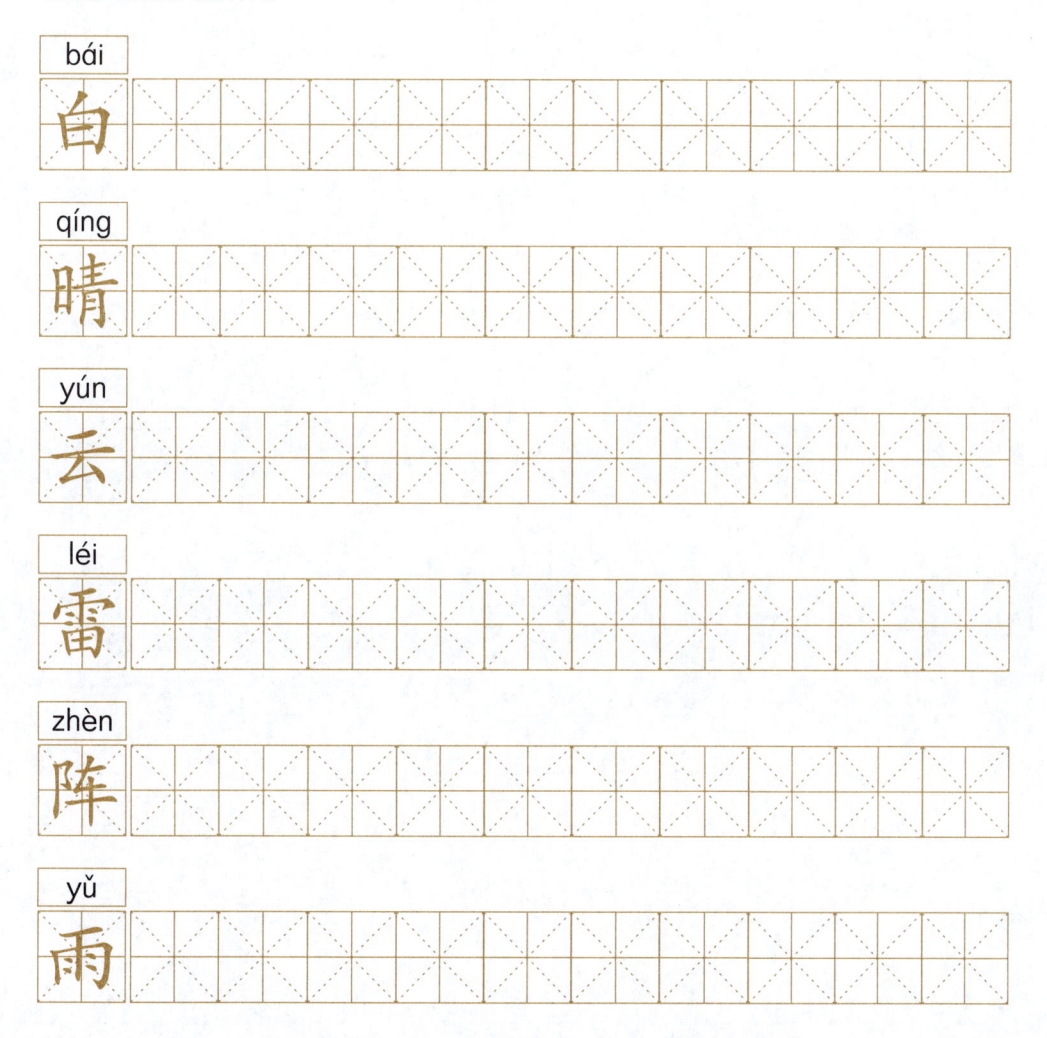

bái
白

qíng
晴

yún
云

léi
雷

zhèn
阵

yǔ
雨

143

| jí |
| 级 |

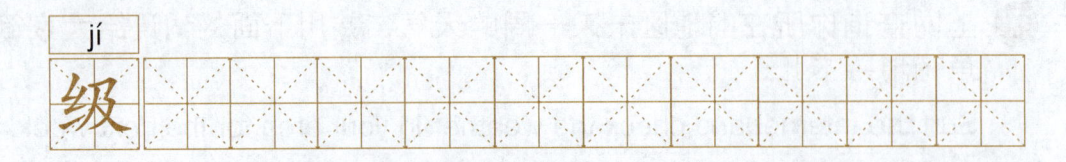

第十三课　汉字笔画笔顺动态图

第十四课 Lesson 14

Jīntiān de qìwēn yǒu duō gāo
今天的气温有多高

重点提示

- 交际功能：谈论气温。
- 主要生词：气温、高、摄氏度、低、零下、下雪、刮风、偏北风、冷。
- 主要语言点：零下，形容词"偏"，副词"有点儿"。
- 文化小常识：全球变暖与环境保护。

一 看图讨论 Look at the picture and discuss

1. 下图是关于什么方面的内容？ What is the following picture about?
2. 他可能在说什么？ What might he say?

145

实用交际汉语 3
Practical Communicative Chinese

二 课文 Text

听录音回答问题 Listen to the recording and answer the following questions.

1. 他们在谈论什么？ What are they talking about?
2. 马文问了一些什么问题？ What questions did Ma Wen ask?
3. 李安平是怎么回答他的？ How did Li Anping answer him?

Jīntiān de qìwēn yǒu duō gāo

今天的气温有多高 🔊 14-1

Mǎ Wén: Jīntiān de qìwēn yǒu duō gāo?
马 文：今天的气温有多高？

Lǐ Ānpíng: Báitiān zuì gāo qìwēn shì wǔ shèshìdù.
李安平：白天最高气温是5摄氏度。

Mǎ Wén: Zuì dī qìwēn shì duōshao?
马 文：最低气温是多少？

Lǐ Ānpíng: Wǎnshang zuì dī qìwēn shì líng xià sān shèshìdù.
李安平：晚上最低气温是零下3摄氏度。

Mǎ Wén: Huì xià xuě ma?
马 文：会下雪吗？

Lǐ Ānpíng: Yǒu xiǎo dào zhōngxuě.
李安平：有小到中雪。

Mǎ Wén: Guā fēng ma?
马 文：刮风吗？

Lǐ Ānpíng: Yǒu sì dào wǔ jí piānběifēng.
李安平：有 4 到 5 级偏北风。

Mǎ Wén: Lěng bu lěng?
马 文：冷 不 冷？

Lǐ Ānpíng: Yǒudiǎnr lěng.
李安平：有点儿冷。

三 生词 New words 14-2

1. 气温	名词	qìwēn	air temperature
2. 高	形容词	gāo	high
3. 摄氏度	量词	shèshìdù	centigrade
度	量词	dù	*a measure word for temperature*
4. 低	形容词	dī	low
5. 零下		líng xià	below zero
零	数词	líng	zero
6. 下雪		xià xuě	snowfall
下	动词	xià	(of rain, snow, etc.) fall
雪	名词	xuě	snow
7. 中雪	名词	zhōngxuě	moderate snow
8. 刮风		guā fēng	blow a gust of wind
刮	动词	guā	blow

9. 偏北风	名词	piānběifēng	northerly wind
偏	形容词	piān	inclined to one side
10. 冷	形容词	lěng	cold
11. 有点儿	副词	yǒudiǎnr	a bit

四 主要语言点 Main language points

1 晚上最低气温是零下 3 摄氏度。

"零下"的意思是温度低于 0 摄氏度，多用来表示天气的温度。例如：

"零下" means that the temperature is below zero degrees Celsius, and it is mostly used to indicate the weather temperature. For example:

（1）今天最低温度是零下 2 摄氏度。
（2）这里的冬天一般是零下 15 摄氏度左右。
（3）零下 5 摄氏度很冷。

▶ 视频：14.1 晚上最低气温是零下 3 摄氏度。

2 有 4 到 5 级偏北风。

这个句子中的"偏"是一个形容词，意思是"不正""不在中间位置"。常常和方位名词"东、南、西、北"组合起来使用，表示方向不是"正东、正南、正西、正北"。天气预报时，常常用来预报风的方向。例如：

"偏" in this sentence is an adjective, meaning "not straight" or "not in the middle". It is often used in combination with nouns of locality, such as "东", "南", "西", and "北" to indicate the direction is not "due east", "due south", "due west" or "due north". In weather forecast, it is often used to forecast the wind direction. For example:

（1）今天有偏南风。
（2）火车站在广州市的偏西方向。
（3）飞机往偏北的方向飞走了。

视频：14.2 有 4 到 5 级偏北风。

3 有点儿冷。

"有点儿"是一个程度副词，表示"稍微、略微"的意思，多表达某种不如意的态度。例如：

"有点儿" is an adverb of degree, which means "slightly". It is mostly used to refer to something unsatisfying. For example:

（1）今天有点儿冷。
（2）老师说话有点儿快。
（3）这个词有点儿难。
（4）这篇课文有点儿长。

视频：14.2 有 4 到 5 级偏北风。

五 文化小常识 General knowledge of culture

全球变暖与环境保护

人体健康与气温的关系非常密切。人体感觉最舒适的环境温度为20～28摄氏度，最有利于人体健康的环境温度在18摄氏度左右。温度过高或过低，都会对人体健康产生不良影响。人们大量使用石油、天然气等物质，由此产生了大量的温室气体，导致全球不断变暖。全球变暖不仅破坏自然生态系统的平衡，造成自然灾害增多，还会威胁人类和动物的生存。所以，人们要联合起来保护自然环境，保护我们的地球。

Global Warming and Environmental Protection

There is a close relationship between human health and temperature. The most comfortable ambient temperature for human body is 20-28 degrees Celsius, and the ambient temperature most conducive to human health is around 18 degrees Celsius. If the temperature is too high or too low, it will have adverse effects on human health. Because of the mass use of oil, natural gas and other substances, a large number of greenhouse gases are produced, which leads to global warming. Global warming not only destroys the balance of natural ecosystem, causing more and more natural disasters, but also threatens the survival of human beings and animals. Therefore, people should jointly protect the natural environment and our planet.

六 》 练习与实践 Exercises and practice

1 听录音，选择你听到的音，然后朗读下面的拼音。 🔊 14-3

Listen to the recording and choose the pronunciation you hear, then read the following Pinyin aloud.

（1）gāo kǎo
    高 — 考

（2）dī tí
    低 — 提

（3）biān piān
    边 — 偏

（4）lěng néng
    冷 — 能

（5）huā guā
    花 — 刮

（6）zhè shè
    这 — 摄

（7）qìwēn jǐ mén
    气温 — 几门

（8）líng xià nǐ xià
    零下 — 你下

（9）dàxué xià xuě
    大学 — 下雪

（10）guā fēng huàfēn
    刮 风 — 划分

（11）shèshìdù zhè shì tú
    摄氏度 — 这是图

（12）biàn měimèng piānběifēng
    变 美梦 — 偏北风

2 朗读下面的句子，注意语调、语气和重音。

Read the following sentences aloud, paying attention to the intonation, tone and stress.

（1）今天的气温有多高？

（2）白天最高气温是5摄氏度。

（3）最低气温是多少？

（4）会下雪吗？

（5）有小到中雪。

（6）有4到5级偏北风。

（7）有点儿冷。

❸ 用汉语读出下面的温度。
Read the temperature shown in the picture below in Chinese.

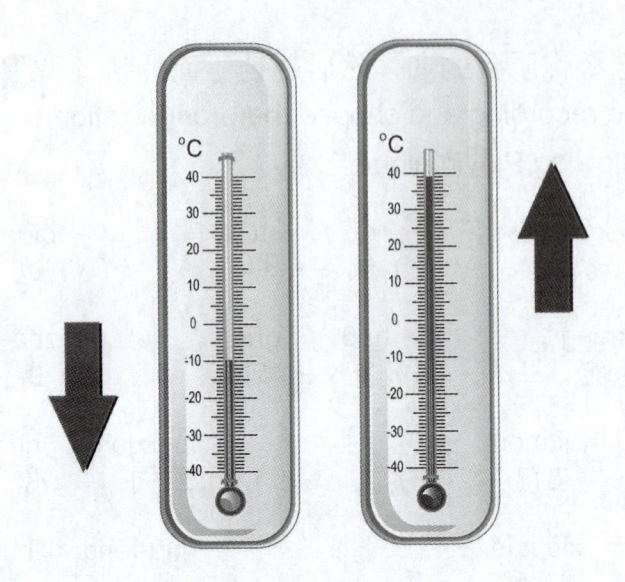

❹ 替换练习：先替换画线的部分，然后和同学一起模仿对话。
Substitution drills: Replace the underlined parts first, then imitate the following dialogue with your classmates.

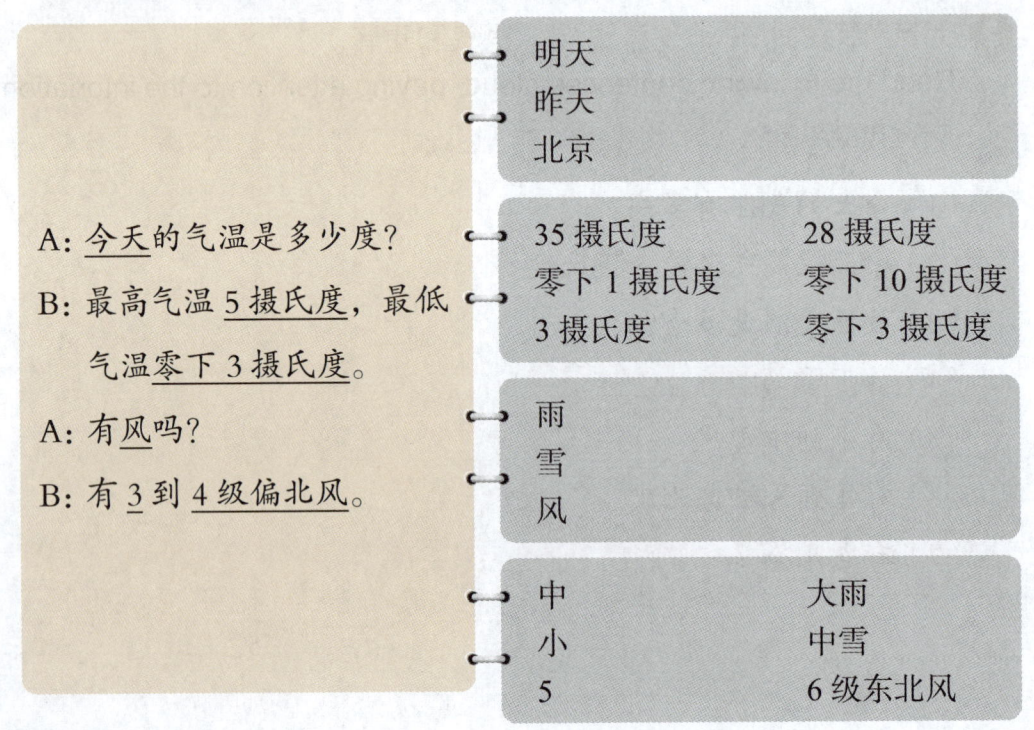

A: <u>今天</u>的气温是多少度？	明天 昨天 北京
B: 最高气温<u>5</u>摄氏度，最低气温<u>零下3</u>摄氏度。	35 摄氏度　　28 摄氏度 零下 1 摄氏度　零下 10 摄氏度 3 摄氏度　　零下 3 摄氏度
A: 有<u>风</u>吗？	雨 雪 风
B: 有<u>3</u>到<u>4</u>级<u>偏北风</u>。	中　　大雨 小　　中雪 5　　6 级东北风

5 看图完成下面的对话，然后和同学一起表演对话的内容。
Look at the pictures and complete the dialogues below, and act them out with your classmates.

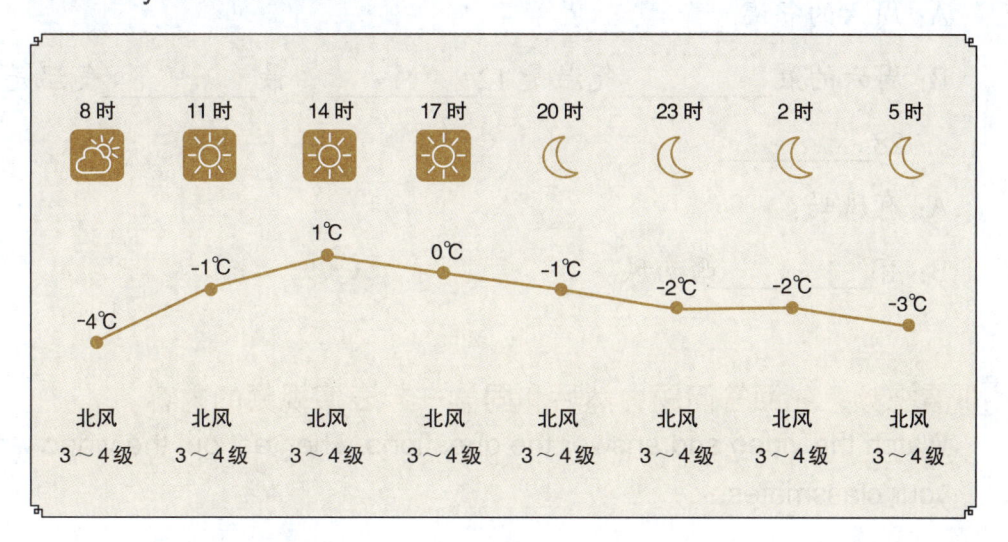

A：今天白天最高_____多少度？

B：白天_____气温是1_____。

A：那晚上_____气温是多少？

B：晚上最低_____是_____ 3 _____。

A：刮_____吗？

B：有_____北风。

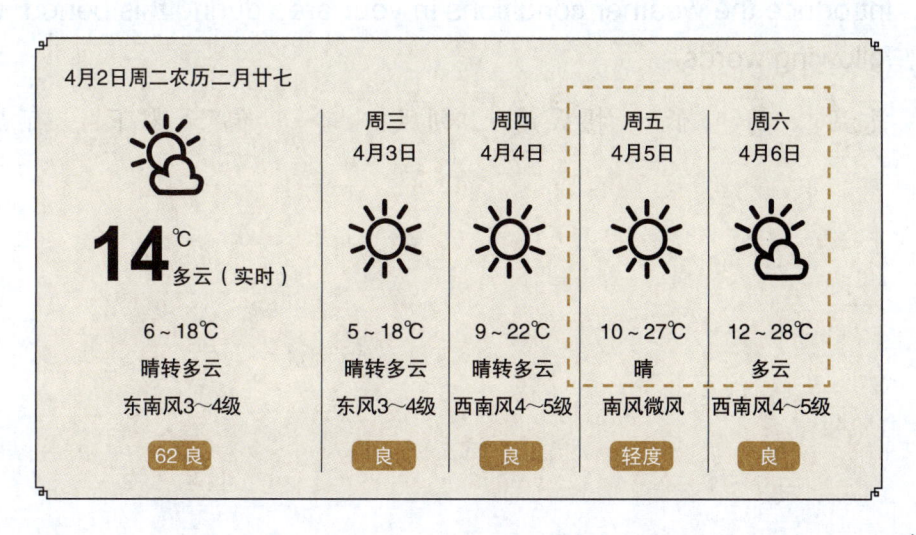

实用交际汉语 3

A: 周四的天气_____?

B: 白天_____。

A: 周六的气温_____?

B: 周六的最_____气温是12_____，最_____气温是28_____。

A: 有风吗?

B: 有_____西南风。

6 看视频，先回答问题，然后和同学一起表演视频的内容。
Watch the video and answer the questions. Then act out the video with your classmates.

（1）男的问了什么问题？

（2）女的是怎么回答的？

> ▶ 视频：14.2 有 4 到 5 级偏北风。

7 用下面的词语介绍一下儿这段时间你所在地区的天气情况。
Introduce the weather conditions in your area during this period with the following words.

气温　高　低　摄氏度　刮风　冷　偏　零下　有点儿

154

8 汉字练习：看汉字笔画笔顺动态图，并跟着书写。
Practice Chinese characters: Look at the animated illustrations of the strokes and the order of strokes of the following characters, and then write them down.

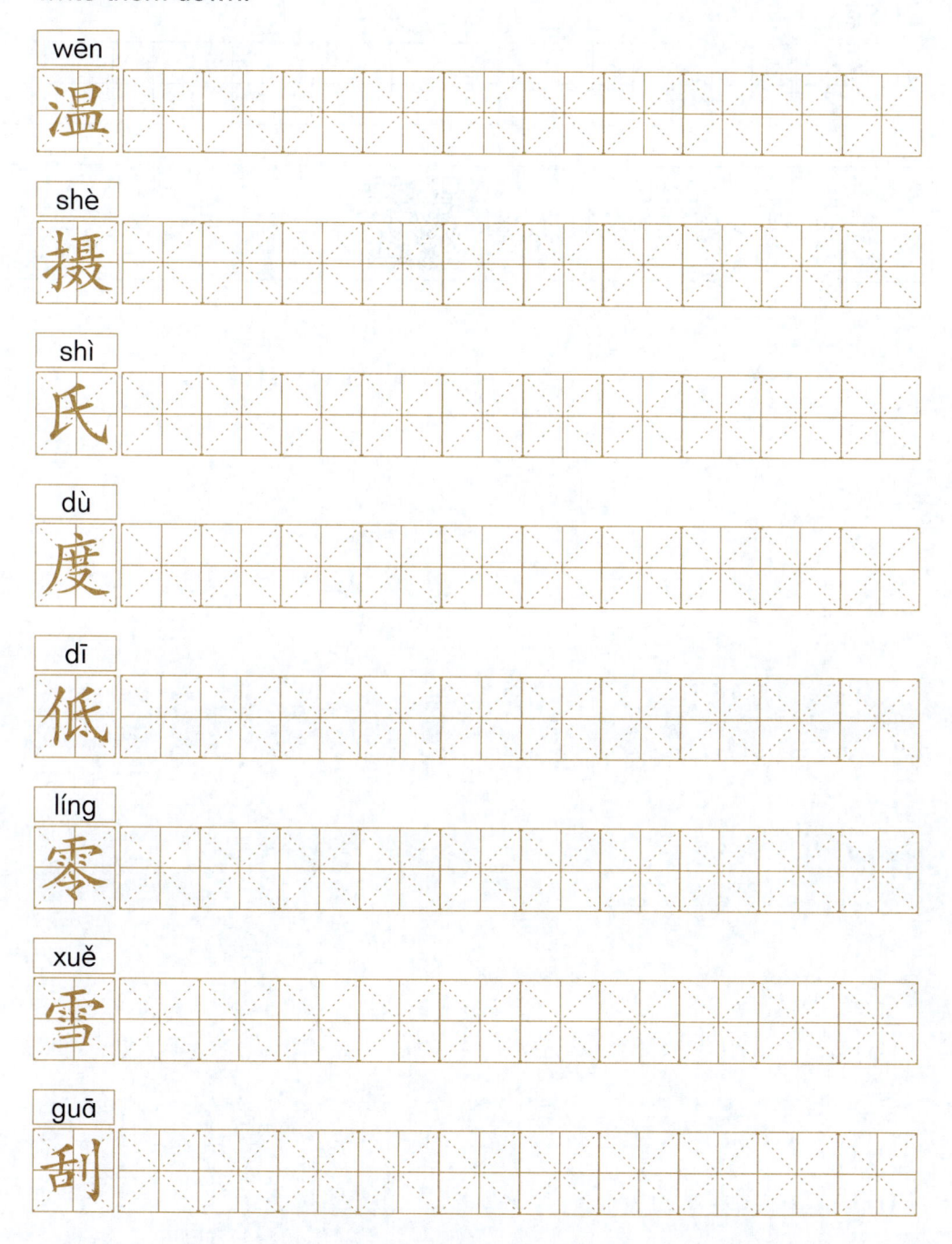

wēn
温

shè
摄

shì
氏

dù
度

dī
低

líng
零

xuě
雪

guā
刮

155

piān
偏

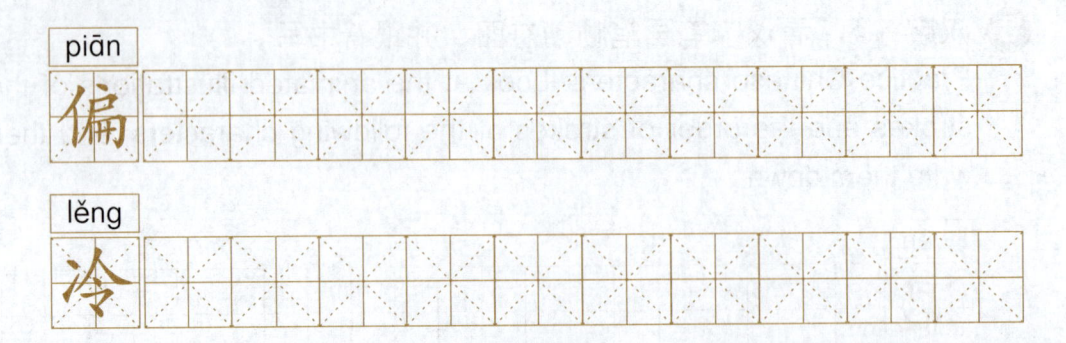

lěng
冷

第十四课　汉字笔画笔顺动态图

第十五课 Lesson 15

Zhōngguó de qìhòu zěnmeyàng
中国的气候怎么样

重点提示

- 交际功能：谈论气候。
- 主要生词：气候、四季、分明、南方、冬天、夏天、热、地方、以上、哪里。
- 主要语言点：不太，以上，句式"比较+形容词/动词"。
- 文化小常识：中国的气候。

一 看图讨论 Look at the picture and discuss

1. 你知道下面左右两张图分别是哪里的冬天吗？ Both the pictures below show somewhere in winter. Do you know where the places are?
2. 你知道为什么两幅图都是冬天而景色却不同呢？ Do you know why both pictures are in winter but the scenery is different?

二 》 课文 Text

听录音回答问题 Listen to the recording and answer the following questions.

1. 他们在谈论什么？ What are they talking about?
2. 马文问了一些什么问题？ What questions did Ma Wen ask?
3. 李安平是怎么回答这些问题的？ How did Li Anping answer these questions?

Zhōngguó de qìhòu zěnmeyàng
中国 的气候怎么样 🔊 15-1

Mǎ Wén: Zhōngguó de qìhòu zěnmeyàng?
马 文： 中国 的气候怎么样？

Lǐ Ānpíng: Zhōngguó de qìhòu hěn hǎo, sìjì fēnmíng.
李安平： 中国 的气候很好，四季分明。

Mǎ Wén: Zhōngguó de nánfāng yě yǒu dōngtiān ma?
马 文： 中国 的南方也有 冬天 吗？

Lǐ Ānpíng: Zhōngguó de nánfāng yě yǒu dōngtiān, dànshì bú tài lěng.
李安平： 中国 的南方也有 冬天，但是不太冷。

Mǎ Wén: Nà xiàtiān rè bu rè?
马 文： 那夏天热不热？

Lǐ Ānpíng: Xiàtiān yǒudiǎnr rè, hěn duō dìfang de qìwēn dōu zài sānshí dù
李安平： 夏天有点儿热，很多地方的气温都在 30 度

yǐshàng.
以上。

158

第十五课　中国的气候怎么样

Mǎ Wén：　Nǐ xǐhuan nǎlǐ de qìhòu?
马　文：　你喜欢哪里的气候？

Lǐ Ānpíng：　Wǒ bǐjiào xǐhuan Zhōngguó nánfāng de qìhòu.
李安平：　我比较喜欢中国南方的气候。

Mǎ Wén：　Nà wǒ yǐhòu qù zhōngguó de nánfāng gōngzuò.
马　文：　那我以后去中国的南方工作。

Lǐ Ānpíng：　Hěn hǎo de dǎsuàn!
李安平：　很好的打算！

三　生词　New words　15-2

1. 气候	名词	qìhòu	climate
2. 四季	名词	sìjì	four seasons
3. 分明	形容词	fēnmíng	clear, obvious
4. 南方	名词	nánfāng	south
5. 冬天	名词	dōngtiān	winter
6. 夏天	名词	xiàtiān	summer
7. 热	形容词	rè	hot
8. 地方	名词	dìfang	place
9. 以上	名词	yǐshàng	being over/above a certain point (in position/order/quantity)
10. 哪里	代词	nǎlǐ	where

四 >> 主要语言点 Main language points

1 中国的南方也有冬天，但是不太冷。

句式"不 + 太 + 形容词/动词"表示减弱否定的程度，交际过程中包含婉转语气。例如：

The sentence pattern "不 + 太 + adjective/verb" means to weaken the degree of negation, which shows a mild and indirect tone in the communication process. For example:

> （1）他的口语不太好。
> （2）马文不太想去。
> （3）小李的考试分数不太高。
> （4）安妮不太爱吃鱼。

视频：15.1 中国的南方也有冬天，但是不太冷。

2 夏天有点儿热，很多地方的气温都在 30 度以上。

"以上"是一个方位名词，基本意思是表示在某一位置的上面，格式是"表位置的词语 + 以上"。例如：

"以上" is a noun of locality. Its basic meaning is to indicate being above a certain position, and the basic pattern it forms is "word indicating position + 以上". For example:

> （1）三楼以上都是客房（kèfáng）。
> （2）云层（céng）以上的空气（kōngqì）很冷。

"以上"还可用于"数量词+以上"格式中，表示大于某个数量。例如：
"以上" can also be used in the pattern "quantifier + 以上", which means being greater than a certain quantity. For example:

（3）今天的最高温度在35度以上。
（4）18岁以上的人都是成年（chéngnián）人。
（5）很多同学考到了90分以上。

▶ 视频：15.2 很多地方的气温都在30度以上。

3 我比较喜欢中国南方的气候。

这句中的"比较"是一个程度副词，表示具有一定的程度，常用于"比较+形容词/动词"格式中。例如：

"比较" in this sentence is an adverb of degree, indicating a certain degree. It is often used in the pattern "比较 + adjective/verb". For example:

（1）我比较喜欢音乐。
（2）王老师比较爱吃广东菜。
（3）今天比较热。
（4）这篇课文比较长。

▶ 视频：15.2 很多地方的气温都在30度以上。

五 文化小常识 General knowledge of culture

中国的气候

中国的气候类型多样，具有明显的大陆性季风气候特点。大部分地区气候温和，四季分明。冬季比较寒冷干燥，夏季比较高温多雨。中国的国土面积广大，因此，不同地区的气候相差也比较大。例如冬季，中国南方地区的平均气温在20度左右，但部分北方地区却低至零下几十度。各地降水量差异也很大，如东南沿海地区的年均降水量达1500毫米以上，而西北地区的年均降水量常常不到200毫米。

The Climate of China

China has a variety of climate types, with obvious characteristics of continental monsoon climate. The climate in most areas is mild with four distinct seasons. It is cold and dry in winter, and hot and rainy in summer. Due to the vast territory of China, the climate in different regions is quite different. For example, in winter, the average temperature in southern China is about 20 degrees Celsius, but in part of northern China, it can be as low as tens of degrees Celsius below zero. There is also a great difference in precipitation. For example, the annual average precipitation in the southeastern coastal area is more than 1,500 millimetres, while that in the northwestern area is often less than 200 millimetres.

六 〉〉 练习与实践 Exercises and practice

1 听录音，选择你听到的音，然后朗读下面的拼音。 🔊 15-3
Listen to the recording and choose the pronunciation you hear, then read the following Pinyin aloud.

（1）jì — qì 　　　　（2）tè — rè 　　　（3）lěng — děng
　　　季 — 气　　　　　　　特 — 热　　　　　　冷 — 等

（4）qìhòu — shíhou　　　　　（5）tōngdiàn — dōngtiān
　　　气候 — 时候　　　　　　　　通电 — 冬天

（6）xiàtiān — jiādiàn　　　　　（7）néng bāng — nánfāng
　　　夏天 — 家电　　　　　　　　能 帮 — 南方

（8）tǐ pàng — dìfang　　　　　（9）yǐshàng — jǐ zhāng
　　　体 胖 — 地方　　　　　　　以上 — 几 张

（10）bǐjiào — dìqiào　　　　　（11）nàlǐ — nǎlǐ
　　　 比较 — 地壳　　　　　　　 那里 — 哪里

2 朗读下面的句子，注意语调、语气和停顿。
Read the following sentences aloud, paying attention to the intonation, tone and pause.

（1）中国的气候怎么样？

（2）中国的气候很好，四季分明。

（3）中国的南方也有冬天吗？

（4）中国的南方也有冬天，但是不太冷。

（5）那夏天热不热？

（6）夏天有点儿热，很多地方的气温都在30度以上。

（7）你喜欢哪里的气候？

（8）我比较喜欢中国南方的气候。

163

实用交际汉语 3
Practical Communicative Chinese

3 连词成句。
Arrange the words to make sentences.

（1）怎么样　的　气候　中国

_____?

（2）南方　也　冬天　吗　中国　的　有

_____?

（3）中国　冷　南方　太　的　不

_____。

（4）气温　都　以上　很　地方　多　在　的　30度

_____。

（5）中国　气候　比较　的　我　南方　喜欢。

_____。

（6）以后　中国　工作　的　南方　我　去

_____。

4 替换练习。
Substitution drills.

（1）<u>中国南方的冬天不太冷</u>。

这篇课文的生词　　难
那里的东西　　　　好
今天的作业　　　　多

164

| （2）很多地方的气温都在30度以上。 | → | 所有学生的成绩　　　　80分
各班的学生人数　　　　20人
各种手机的价格（jiàgé）　3000块 |

| （3）我比较喜欢南方的气候。 | → | 他　　　喜欢吃北京菜
马文　　想去北京旅游
小李　　爱听中文歌 |

5 用下面的词语介绍一下儿你去过的中国某个地方的气候特点。
Introduce the climate characteristics of a place in China you have been to with the following words.

气候　季　冷　热　比较　以上　地方　不太

6 两至三人一组，讨论一下儿自己喜欢的天气及其理由。
Work in groups of two or three, and discuss your favourite weather and explain why.

7 看视频，先回答问题，然后和同学一起表演视频的内容。
Watch the video and answer the questions. Then act out the video with your classmates.

（1）根据视频，中国南方的夏天热吗？气温一般是多少？
（2）女的喜欢哪里的气候呢？

▶ 视频：15.3 中国的南方也有冬天吗？

8 汉字练习：看汉字笔画笔顺动态图，并跟着书写。

Practice Chinese characters: Look at the animated illustrations of the strokes and the order of strokes of the following characters, and then write them down.

sì
四

jì
季

dōng
冬

xià
夏

rè
热

第十五课　汉字笔画笔顺动态图

交际项目五
谈论旅游

第十六课 Lesson 16

Wǒmen chūqù jiāoyóu ba
我们出去郊游吧

重点提示

- 交际功能：讨论郊游安排。
- 主要生词：出去、郊游、景区、美、出发、上山、步行、待会儿。
- 主要语言点：复合趋向动词"出去"，格式"动词+补语+就+动词……"，数量词"一会儿"。
- 文化小常识：5A 景区。

一 》》看图讨论 Look at the picture and discuss

1. 他们可能在做什么？What might they be doing?
2. 他们可能说什么呢？What might they say?

168

二 》 课 文 Text

听录音回答问题 Listen to the recording and answer the following questions.

1. 他们在谈论什么？ What are they talking about?
2. 马文问了一些什么问题？ What questions did Ma Wen ask?
3. 李安平是怎么回答这些问题的？ How did Li Anping answer these questions?

Wǒmen chūqù jiāoyóu ba
我们出去郊游吧 🔊 16-1

Mǎ Wén： Jīntiān de tiānqì zhēn hǎo!
马　文： 今天的天气真好！

Lǐ Ānpíng： Kěbúshi!
李安平： 可不是！

Mǎ Wén： Wǒmen chūqù jiāoyóu ba.
马　文： 我们出去郊游吧。

Lǐ Ānpíng： Hǎo a!
李安平： 好啊！

Mǎ Wén： Wǒmen qù nǎr jiāoyóu ne?
马　文： 我们去哪儿郊游呢？

Lǐ Ānpíng： Wǒmen fùjìn de Báiyún Shān shì 5A jǐngqū, fēngjǐng hěn měi.
李安平： 我们附近的白云山是5A景区，风景很美。

　　　　　Nǐ juéde zěnmeyàng?
　　　　　你觉得怎么样？

Mǎ Wén:	Nàlǐ de fēngjǐng shì méideshuō! Wǒ yě hěn xǐhuan nàr.
马 文:	那里的风景是没的说！我也很喜欢那儿。

Lǐ Ānpíng:	Wǒmen shénme shíhou chūfā?
李安平:	我们 什么 时候 出发？

Mǎ Wén:	Wǒmen chīwán zǎocān jiù chūfā, zěnmeyàng?
马 文:	我们 吃完 早餐 就 出发，怎么样？

Lǐ Ānpíng:	Méi wèntí.
李安平:	没 问题。

Mǎ Wén:	Wǒmen zěnme shàngshān ne?
马 文:	我们 怎么 上山 呢？

Lǐ Ānpíng:	Wǒmen bùxíng shàngshān ba.
李安平:	我们 步行 上山 吧。

Mǎ Wén:	Hǎo, yíhuìr jiàn!
马 文:	好，一会儿见！

Lǐ Ānpíng:	Dāihuìr jiàn!
李安平:	待会儿见！

三 》 生 词 New words 16-2

1. 出去	动词	chūqù	go out
2. 郊游	动词	jiāoyóu	picnic
3. 白云山	专有名词	Báiyún Shān	Baiyun Mountain

4. 景区	名词	jǐngqū	scenic area
5. 美	形容词	měi	beautiful
6. 出发	动词	chūfā	set out/off
7. 完	动词	wán	finish
8. 早餐	名词	zǎocān	breakfast
9. 上山	动词	shàngshān	climb a mountain
10. 步行	动词	bùxíng	walk
11. 一会儿	数量词	yíhuìr	a moment
12. 待会儿		dāihuìr	after a while, later
待	动词	dāi	wait

四 主要语言点 Main language points

1 我们出去游郊吧。

"出去"是由动词"出"与趋向动词"去"组成的一个复合趋向动词，表示动作离开说话人所在地。"出去"可以用于已经发生的情况，也可以用于将要发生的情况。例如：

"出去" is a compound directional verb composed of the verb "出" and the directional verb "去", which indicates that the speaker leaves where he/she was. It can be used for situations that have already occurred or that are about to occur. For example:

171

（1）我们出去吃饭吧。
（2）他还没有出去。
（3）老师出去开会了。
（4）妈妈出去旅游了。

▶ 视频：16.1 我们出去郊游吧。

❷ 我们吃完早餐就出发，怎么样？

这句中的"就"是一个副词，用在两个动词之间，构成"动词＋补语＋就＋动词……"的格式，表示两个动作连续发生，中间的时间间隔很短。例如：

"就" in this sentence is an adverb, which is used between two verbs to form the pattern "verb + complement + 就 + verb...", indicating that two actions occur continuously with a short time interval. For example:

（1）我做完作业就去找你。
（2）他拿了手机就出去了。
（3）老师上完课就走了。
（4）我们考完就放假。

▶ 视频：16.2 我们吃完早餐就出发。

❸ 好，一会儿见！

"一会儿"是数量词，指很短的时间。"一会儿见"是一句常用的客套话，指参与交际的谈话人结束此次谈话后会在很短的时间内再次见面。例如：

"一会儿" is a quantifier, which refers to a short period of time. "一会儿见" is a frequently-used polite expression. It means that the speakers will meet again in a short time after this conversation. For example:

（1）A: 我上完课就来!
　　　B: 好, 一会儿见!
（2）A: 我在地铁上, 很快就到!
　　　B: 好的, 一会儿见!

▶ 视频：16.3 一会儿见!

五 文化小常识 General knowledge of culture

5A 景区

　　5A 景区是 AAAAA 级旅游景区的简称。中国的旅游景区一般根据其质量水平划分为五个等级，从高到低依次为 5A、4A、3A、2A、1A 级。其中，5A 级为最高等级。截至 2022 年 7 月，中国国家文旅部共确定了 318 家国家 5A 级旅游风景区，如北京的长城、故宫，浙江杭州的西湖，四川的九寨沟，湖北的武当山，山东的泰山，江西的井冈山，广东的白云山，广西桂林的漓江等都是非常有名的 5A 景区。

5A Scenic Area

5A scenic area is the abbreviation of AAAAA-level tourist attractions. China's tourist attractions usually fall into five levels based on their quality, with 5A, 4A, 3A, 2A, and 1A levels in descending order. Among them, 5A is considered the highest. As of July 2022, Ministry of Culture and Tourism of China has identified 318 national 5A tourist attractions, such as the Great Wall and the Imperial Palace in Beijing, the West Lake in Hangzhou, Zhejiang Province, Jiuzhaigou in Sichuan Province, Mount Wudang in Hubei Province, Mount Tai in Shandong Province, Mount Jinggang in Jiangxi Province, Mount Baiyun in Guangdong Province, Lijiang in Guilin, Guangxi Zhuang Autonomous Region, and so on.

第十六课　我们出去郊游吧

六　练习与实践 Exercises and practice

1 听录音，选择你听到的音，然后朗读下面的拼音。 🔊 16-3

Listen to the recording and choose the pronunciation you hear, then read the following Pinyin aloud.

（1）jǐng — qǐng
　　景 — 请

（2）qū — qǔ
　　区 — 曲

（3）qiāo — jiāo
　　敲 — 郊

（4）chū — shū
　　出 — 书

（5）shān — cān
　　山 — 餐

（6）dāi — tài
　　待 — 太

（7）chūqù — zǔ jù
　　出去 — 组句

（8）jiāoyóu — xiǎo qiú
　　郊游 — 小球

（9）qíngxù — jǐngqū
　　情绪 — 景区

（10）shàngshān — Zhāng Sān
　　　上山 — 张三

（11）bùxíng — bùjǐng
　　　步行 — 布景

（12）cǎo shān — zǎocān
　　　草山 — 早餐

2 朗读下面的句子，注意语调、语气和停顿。

Read the following sentences aloud, paying attention to the intonation, tone and pause.

（1）今天的天气真好！

（2）我们出去郊游吧。

（3）我们去哪儿郊游呢？

（4）我们附近的白云山是5A景区，风景很美。

（5）那里的风景是没的说！

（6）我们什么时候出发？

（7）我们吃完早餐就出发，怎么样？

175

实用交际汉语 3
Practical Communicative Chinese

3 用汉语说出下列图片中景区的名称，并简单介绍一下儿它所在的位置和特色。
Tell the name of each scenic spot in the pictures below and briefly introduce their locations and characteristics in Chinese.

（1）

（2）

（3）

4 替换练习。
Substitution drills.

(1) 我们出去<u>郊游</u>吧。
　　吃饭
　　购物
　　买书

(2) 我们<u>吃完早餐</u>就<u>出发</u>。
　　做完作业　　睡觉
　　上完课　　　过来
　　考完试　　　回家

(3) <u>那里的风景</u>是没的说。
　　我们的校园环境
　　王老师的课
　　昨天的晚会

5 根据语境完成下面的对话，然后和同学一起表演对话的内容。
Complete the following dialogues based on the language context and act them out with your classmates.

（老师在课堂上点名）

(1) 老师：马文怎么没有来？
　　同学A：老师，他来了，刚刚＿＿＿＿＿＿了。

（学生到办公室找王老师）

(2) 学生：请问王老师在吗？
　　老师A：王老师＿＿＿＿＿＿开会了。

（两人在打电话）

(3) A：我们等你很久啦！
　　B：我拿＿＿＿＿＿＿衣服＿＿＿＿＿＿过来。

（考试要结束了）

（4）老师：交卷儿（juànr）！

学生A：好的，我写_____学号_____交。

6 两至三人一组，用下面的词语讨论一下儿去某个景区的旅游计划。
Work in groups of two or three, and discuss your plan of travelling to some scenic spot with the following words.

出发　景区　风景　美　就　步行　一会儿见

7 看视频，先回答问题，然后自己用汉语介绍一下儿这个景区。
Watch the video and answer the questions. Then introduce the scenic spot in Chinese.

（1）他们什么时候出发？

（2）他们怎么上山？

▶ 视频：16.4 我们什么时候出发？

8 汉字练习：看汉字笔画笔顺动态图，并跟着书写。
Practice Chinese characters: Look at the animated illustrations of the strokes and the order of strokes of the following characters, and then write them down.

jiāo
郊

qū
区

wán
完

cān
餐

dāi
待

第十六课　汉字笔画笔顺动态图

第十七课 Lesson 17

Nǐ juéde gēntuányóu zěnmeyàng
你觉得跟团游怎么样

重点提示

- 交际功能：谈论跟团游。
- 主要生词：跟团游、优点、吃饭、住宿、操心、缺点、游玩、自由、老人、如果。
- 主要语言点：副词"最好"，疑问句"……多吗"，表示假设的"的话"。
- 文化小常识：跟团游。

一 看图讨论 Look at the picture and discuss

1. 他们可能在做什么？What might they be doing?
2. 他们可能说什么呢？What might they say?

二 课文 Text

听录音回答问题 Listen to the recording and answer the following questions.

1. 他们在谈论什么？ What are they talking about?
2. 马文问了一些什么问题？ What questions did Ma Wen ask?
3. 李安平是怎么回答这些问题的？ How did Li Anping answer these questions?

Nǐ juéde gēntuányóu zěnmeyàng
你觉得跟团游怎么样 17-1

Mǎ Wén： Nǐ juéde gēntuányóu zěnmeyàng?
马　文： 你觉得跟团游怎么样？

Lǐ Ānpíng： Tā de zuì dà yōudiǎn shì bǐjiào fāngbiàn, chīfàn、 zhùsù děng dōu
李安平： 它的最大优点是比较方便，吃饭、住宿等都

búyòng zìjǐ cāoxīn.
不用自己操心。

Mǎ Wén： Nà tā de quēdiǎn ne?
马　文： 那它的缺点呢？

Lǐ Ānpíng： Tā de quēdiǎn zhǔyào shì yóuwán bú tài zìyóu.
李安平： 它的缺点主要是游玩不太自由。

Mǎ Wén： Nǎxiē rén bǐjiào shìhé gēntuányóu ne?
马　文： 哪些人比较适合跟团游呢？

Lǐ Ānpíng: Yìbān lái shuō, lǎorén zuìhǎo xuǎnzé gēntuányóu.
李安平：一般来说，老人最好选择跟团游。

Mǎ Wén: Xiànzài cānjiā gēntuányóu de rén duō ma?
马 文：现在参加跟团游的人多吗？

Lǐ Ānpíng: Hěn duō.
李安平：很多。

Mǎ Wén: Wǒ rúguǒ qù lǚyóu dehuà, yě cānjiā gēntuányóu.
马 文：我如果去旅游的话，也参加跟团游。

三 ▶ 生词 New words 🔊 17-2

1. 跟团游	名词	gēntuányóu	group tour
2. 优点	名词	yōudiǎn	merit, virtue
3. 吃饭	动词	chīfàn	dining
饭	名词	fàn	meal
4. 住宿	动词	zhùsù	stay, put up
5. 操心	动词	cāoxīn	worry about
6. 缺点	名词	quēdiǎn	disadvantage
7. 游玩	动词	yóuwán	go sightseeing, visit
8. 自由	形容词	zìyóu	free
9. 一般来说		yìbān lái shuō	in general

10. 老人	名词	lǎorén	the aged
11. 最好	副词	zuìhǎo	had better
12. 选择	动词	xuǎnzé	choose
13. 如果	连词	rúguǒ	if
14. 的话	助词	dehuà	an auxiliary word used after a hypothetical clause

四 主要语言点 Main language points

1 一般来说,老人最好选择跟团游。

这句中的"最好"是一个副词,表示最理想、最适当的选择。交际中多用于提出某项建议,语气较为温和。例如:

"最好" in this sentence is an adverb, which means the most ideal and the most appropriate choice. In communication, it is often used to make a suggestion in a mild tone. For example:

(1)今天可能(kěnéng)有雨,你最好带上雨伞(yǔsǎn)。
(2)下个星期就要考试了,你最好提前复习一下儿。
(3)这件(jiàn)事你最好和父母(fùmǔ)说一下儿。

▶ 视频:17.1 一般来说,老人最好选择跟团游。

② 现在参加跟团游的人多吗?

这是由形容词"多"与"吗"放于句尾而构成的疑问句,主要用来询问某种情况出现的数量或者程度。类似的形容词还有"大、远、愉快"等,相当于询问"……A 不 A"。例如:

This is an interrogative sentence composed of the adjective "多" and "吗" at the end of the sentence, which is used to inquire the number or degree of a situation. Similar adjectives also include "大", "远", "愉快", etc., which is equivalent to "……A 不 A". For example:

(1)现在学汉语的人多吗?
(2)你们班的泰国学生多吗?
(3)飞机场离我们学校远吗?
(4)这次旅游玩儿得愉快吗?

▷ 视频:17.2 现在参加跟团游的人多吗?

③ 我如果去旅游的话,也参加跟团游。

汉语中,"的话"用在表示假设的分句后,表示假设语气,后一分句表示在假设情况下产生的结果。"的话"可与"如果"搭配使用,也可单独使用。例如:

In Chinese, "的话" is used after a hypothetical clause to indicate a hypothetical tone. The clause followed shows the result under the hypothetical situation. "的话" can either be used together with "如果" or independently. For example:

(1)你如果不想去的话,可以不去。
(2)明天如果下雨的话,大家可以不来。
(3)这次如果没有你帮忙的话,我真的不知道该怎么办。

（4）我没有课的话，就参加比赛。

（5）同学们有问题的话，可以问老师。

▶ 视频：17.2 现在参加跟团游的人多吗？

五 文化小常识 General knowledge of culture

跟团游

跟团游是指个人跟着旅行社组织的团队一起去旅游，一般分为全跟团和半跟团两种。全跟团是指整个旅游过程中的各项活动计划都由旅行社负责，游客全程听从旅行社的安排。半跟团是指旅行社负责整个旅游过程中的某一项或某几项活动计划，游客可以有部分自由活动的时间。一般老人、小孩儿和出国游可以选择全跟团；国内游，特别是去比较熟悉的地方则可以选择半跟团。

Group Tour

Taking a group tour refers to travelling with a group organised by a travel agency. It is usually divided into two types: full-group tour and semi-group tour. Full-group tour means that the travel agency is responsible for all the activities throughout the journey, and tourists follow the travel agency's arrangements. Semi-group tour refers to the travel agency is responsible for one or several activities in the trip, and tourists can have some free time. The elderly, children and those who travel abroad are suggested to choose full-group tour. However, for people taking domestic tours, especially tours to familiar places, taking a semi-group tour is a good choice.

六 练习与实践 Exercises and practice

1 听录音，选择你听到的音，然后朗读下面的拼音。 🔊 17-3
Listen to the recording and choose the pronunciation you hear, then read the following Pinyin aloud.

（1）fèn duàn — gēntuán
　　　分　段 — 跟团

（2）yōudiǎn — qiūtiān
　　　优点 — 秋天

（3）cāoxīn — zǎo jìn
　　　操心 — 早　进

（4）xuě tiān — quēdiǎn
　　　雪　天 — 缺点

（5）chíjiǔ — zìyóu
　　　持久 — 自由

（6）zhùsù — chū shū
　　　住宿 — 出　书

（7）zuìhǎo — shuìzháo
　　　最好 — 睡着

（8）quán cè — xuǎnzé
　　　全　册 — 选择

2 朗读下面的句子，注意语调、语气和停顿。
Read the following sentences aloud, paying attention to the intonation, tone and pause.

（1）你觉得跟团游怎么样？

（2）它的最大优点是比较方便，吃饭、住宿等都不用自己操心。

（3）哪些人比较适合跟团游呢？

（4）一般来说，老人最好选择跟团游。

（5）现在参加跟团游的人多吗？

（6）我如果去旅游的话，也参加跟团游。

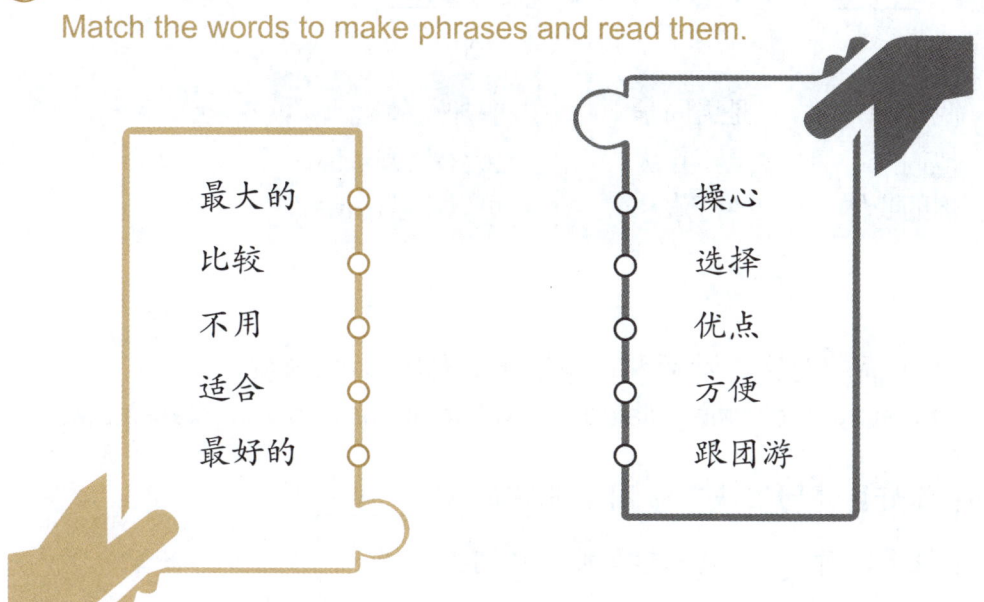

❸ 连线组成短语，并读一读。
Match the words to make phrases and read them.

最大的　　　　　操心
比较　　　　　　选择
不用　　　　　　优点
适合　　　　　　方便
最好的　　　　　跟团游

❹ 替换练习：先替换画线的部分，然后和同学一起模仿对话。
Substitution drills: Replace the underlined parts first, then imitate the following dialogues with your classmates.

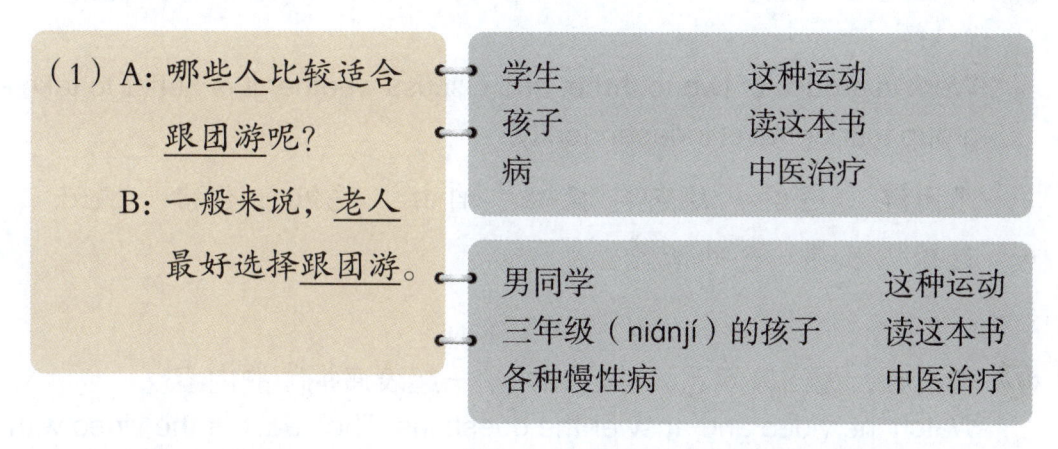

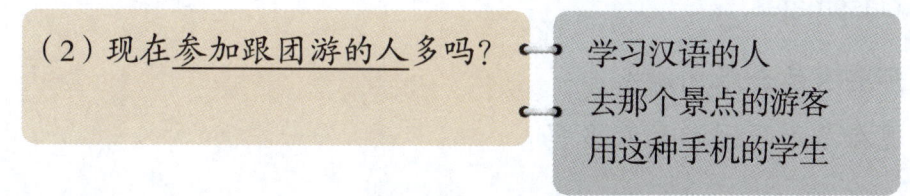

（1）A：哪些<u>人</u>比较适合<u>跟团游</u>呢？
　　　B：一般来说，<u>老人</u>最好选择<u>跟团游</u>。

学生　　　　　这种运动
孩子　　　　　读这本书
病　　　　　　中医治疗

男同学　　　　　　　　这种运动
三年级（niánjí）的孩子　读这本书
各种慢性病　　　　　　中医治疗

（2）现在<u>参加跟团游的人</u>多吗？

学习汉语的人
去那个景点的游客
用这种手机的学生

187

（3）<u>我</u>下次如果<u>去旅游</u>的话也<u>参加跟团游</u>。

我	是男同学	参加这种运动
他们	上三年级	会喜欢读这本书
你的身体	不舒服	可以用中医治疗

5 完成下面的对话，然后和同学一起表演对话的内容。
Complete the following dialogue, and act it out with your classmates.

A：你好！请问国庆节跟团去北京的人＿＿＿＿？

B：很多。你＿＿＿＿选择别的假期去。

A：＿＿＿＿选择别的时间＿＿＿＿，什么时候最＿＿＿＿呢？

B：十月下旬或者十一月上旬都比较＿＿＿＿。

6 两至三人一组，用下面的词语讨论一下儿参加跟团游好还是自由行好。
Work in groups of two to three, and discuss whether it is better to take a group tour or travel independently.

跟团游　适合　缺点　操心　自由　吃饭　住宿　最好
选择　如果……的话

7 看视频，先回答问题，然后和同学一起表演视频的内容。
Watch the video and answer the questions. Then act out the video with your classmates.

（1）哪些人适合跟团游？

（2）现在参加跟团游的人多吗？

（3）男的以后准备怎么做？

▶ 视频：17.3 哪些人比较适合跟团游呢？

❽ 汉字练习：看汉字笔画笔顺动态图，并跟着书写。
Practice Chinese characters: Look at the animated illustrations of the strokes and the order of strokes of the following characters, and then write them down.

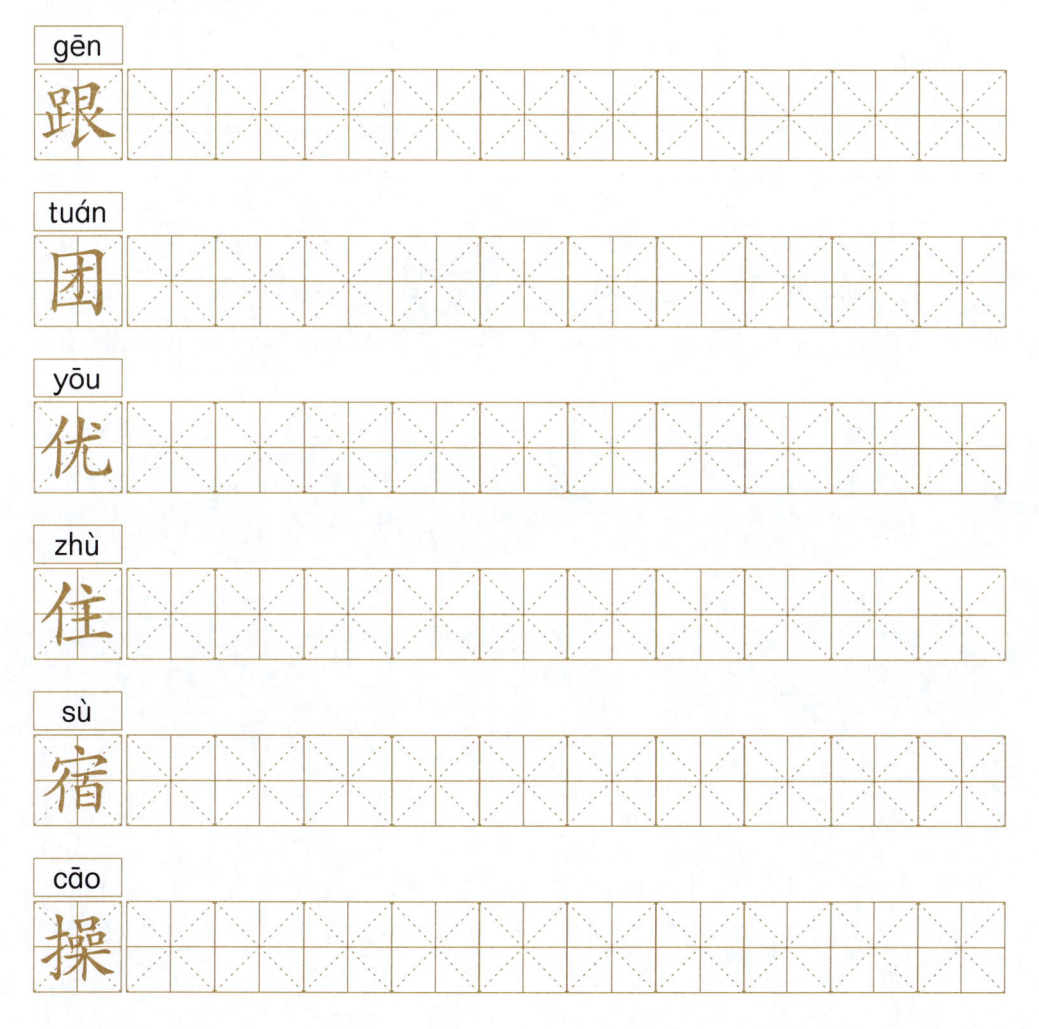

gēn
跟

tuán
团

yōu
优

zhù
住

sù
宿

cāo
操

quē
缺

xuǎn
选

zé
择

huà
话

第十七课　汉字笔画笔顺动态图

第十八课 Lesson 18

Wǒ dǎsuàn cānjiā chūjìngyóu
我打算参加出境游

重点提示

- **交际功能**：谈论出境游。
- **主要生词**：出境游、五一、景点、热情、好客、旅途。
- **主要语言点**：副词"马上"，格式"要+动词+了"。
- **文化小常识**：出境游。

一 看图讨论 Look at the picture and discuss

1. 他们可能在做什么？ What might they be doing?
2. 他们可能说什么呢？ What might they say?

191

二 》 课 文 Text

听录音回答问题 Listen to the recording and answer the following questions.

1. 他们在谈论什么？ What are they talking about?
2. 马文问了一些什么问题？ What questions did Ma Wen ask?
3. 李安平是怎么回答这些问题的？ How did Li Anping answer these questions?

Wǒ dǎsuàn cānjiā chūjìngyóu
我打算参加出境游 🔊 18-1

Mǎ Wén: "Wǔ-Yī" mǎshàng yào dào le, nǐ yǒu shénme dǎsuàn ma?
马 文： "五一"马上 要 到 了，你 有 什么 打算 吗？

Lǐ Ānpíng: Wǒ dǎsuàn cānjiā chūjìngyóu.
李安平： 我 打算 参加 出境游。

Mǎ Wén: Nǐ dǎsuàn qù nǎge guójiā ne?
马 文： 你 打算 去 哪个 国家 呢？

Lǐ Ānpíng: Wǒ dǎsuàn qù Tàiguó.
李安平： 我 打算 去 泰国。

Mǎ Wén: Wèi shénme xuǎnzé Tàiguó ne?
马 文： 为 什么 选择 泰国 呢？

Lǐ Ānpíng: Tàiguó de lǚyóu jǐngdiǎn duō, Tàiguórén yě hěn rèqíng hàokè.
李安平： 泰国 的 旅游 景点 多，泰国人 也 很 热情 好客。

Mǎ Wén: Nǐ dǎsuàn qù nǎxiē dìfang ne?
马 文： 你 打算 去 哪些 地方 呢？

Lǐ Ānpíng： Wǒ dǎsuàn qù Màngǔ、 Pǔjí Dǎo děng dìfang.
李安平： 我打算去曼谷、普吉岛 等 地方。

Mǎ Wén： Zhù nǐ lǚtú yúkuài!
马 文： 祝你旅途愉快！

Lǐ Ānpíng： Xièxie!
李安平： 谢谢！

三 生词 New words 18-2

1. 出境游	名词	chūjìngyóu	outbound tourism
出境	动词	chūjìng	leave a certain district, county, province. etc.
2. 五一	专有名词	Wǔ-Yī	May 1st, International Labour Day
3. 马上	副词	mǎshàng	immediately
4. 要	助动词	yào	be going to, be about to
5. 景点	名词	jǐngdiǎn	scenic spot
6. 热情	形容词	rèqíng	enthusiastic, warm-hearted
7. 好客	形容词	hàokè	hospitable
8. 普吉岛	专有名词	Pǔjí Dǎo	Phuket
9. 旅途	名词	lǚtú	journey

四 主要语言点 Main language points

1 "五一"马上要到了，你有什么打算吗?

"马上"是一个时间副词，常用在动词前面，构成"马上 + 动词"的格式，表示某事将在很短的时间内发生。例如：

"马上" is an adverb of time. It is often used before a verb to form the pattern "马上 + verb", which means that something will happen in a short period of time. For example:

(1) 我马上去。
(2) 你马上来我办公室一下儿。
(3) 车子马上到。
(4) 考试马上结束。

这句中的"要"是一个助动词，用在动词前，句末常常加"了"，构成"要 + 动词 + 了"的格式，表示某事将要发生或某种情况将要出现。例如：

"要" in this sentence is an auxiliary verb used before a verb. "了" is often added at the end of a sentence to form the pattern "要 + verb + 了", indicating that something or some situation is about to happen. For example:

(5) 天要下雨了。
(6) 学校快(kuài)要放假了。
(7) 我们要考试了。
(8) 四年级的同学很快就要毕业了。

格式"要 + 动词 + 了"前面常常加副词"马上"，构成句式"马上 + 要 + 动词 + 了"，表示某事将在很短的时间内发生或某种情况将在很短的时间内出现。例如：

The pattern "要 + verb + 了" is often preceded by the adverb "马上" to form the sentence pattern "马上 + 要 + verb + 了", meaning that something or some situation is about to happen soon. For example:

（9）车子马上要到了，你快点儿。
（10）我们马上要考试了，大家都在认真复习。
（11）飞机马上要起飞了，大家再见。
（12）比赛马上要开始了，同学们加油（jiāyóu）。

视频：18.1 "五一" 马上要到了，你有什么打算吗？

五 文化小常识 General knowledge of culture

出境游

出境游是旅游的一种，指旅游者到其他国家或境外地区去旅游，比如中国人去泰国、美国、英国等地旅游度假。2019年，中国的出境旅游规模达到1.55亿人次，出境游客境外消费超过1338亿美元。泰国的旅游资源非常丰富，又有独具特色的佛教文化，还有世界有名的泰拳。因此，泰国连续多年成为中国出境旅游人数最多的目的地国家之一。

Outbound Tourism

Outbound tourism is a type of tourism, which refers to tourists travelling to countries or regions outside the borders. For example, Chinese people travel to Thailand, the United States, the United Kingdom and other places for vacation. In 2019, the number of Chinese outbound tourists reached 155 million, and the overseas consumption of outbound tourists exceeded 133.8 billion U.S. dollars. With abundant tourist resources, unique Buddhist culture, and world-famous Muay Thai, Thailand has been one of the top destination countries for Chinese outbound tourists for many years.

六 练习与实践 Exercises and practice

1 听录音，选择你听到的音，然后朗读下面的拼音。 18-3
Listen to the recording and choose the pronunciation you hear, then read the following Pinyin aloud.

(1) 哪张 — 马上
   nǎ zhāng mǎshàng

(2) 热情 — 特性
   rèqíng tèxìng

(3) 好客 — 好歌
   hàokè hǎo gē

(4) 女友 — 旅途
   nǚyǒu lǚtú

(5) 大段 — 打算
   dà duàn dǎsuàn

(6) 出境 — 去请
   chūjìng qù qǐng

(7) 出境游 — 去请求
   chūjìngyóu qù qǐngqiú

(8) 不知道 — 普吉岛
   bù zhīdào Pǔjí Dǎo

2 朗读下面的句子，注意语调、语气和停顿。
Read the following sentences aloud, paying attention to the intonation, tone and pause.

（1）"五一"马上要到了，你有什么打算吗？

（2）我打算参加出境游。

（3）你打算去哪个国家呢？

（4）我打算去泰国。

（5）你打算去哪些地方呢？

（6）我打算去曼谷、普吉岛等地方。

（7）祝你旅途愉快！

3 替换练习。
Substitution drills.

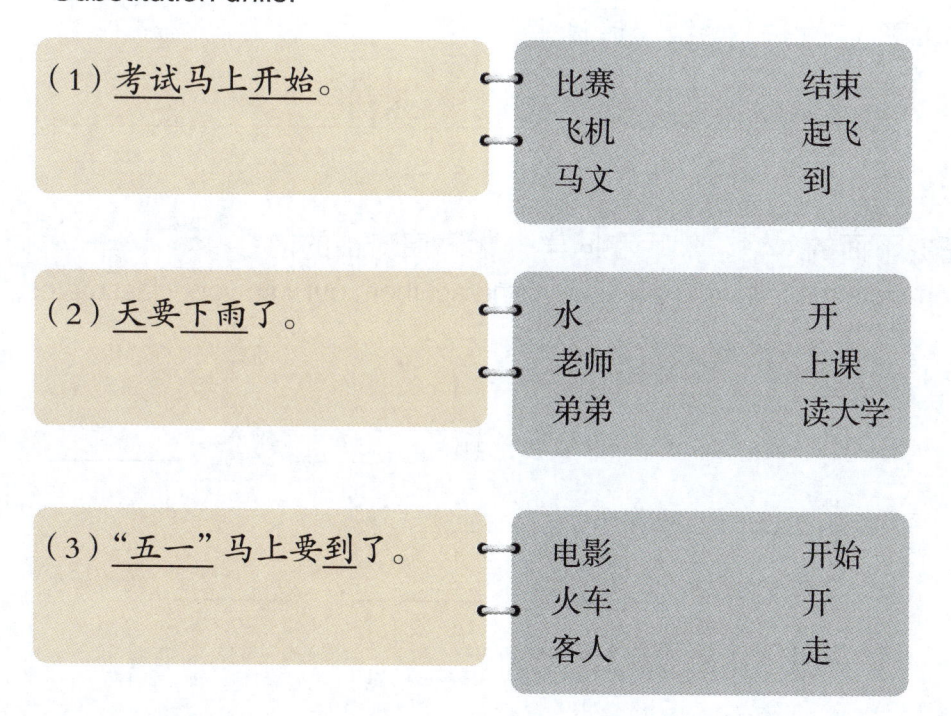

（1）<u>考试</u>马上<u>开始</u>。

比赛	结束
飞机	起飞
马文	到

（2）<u>天</u>要<u>下雨</u>了。

水	开
老师	上课
弟弟	读大学

（3）"<u>五一</u>"马上要<u>到</u>了。

电影	开始
火车	开
客人	走

❹ 连词成句。
Arrange the words to make sentences.

（1）打算　出境游　我　参加

　　_____。

（2）景点　泰国　多　旅游　的　很

　　_____。

（3）好客　也　热情　很　泰国人

　　_____。

（4）哪些　你　去　旅游　地方　打算

　　_____？

（5）祝　愉快　你　旅途

　　_____！

❺ 完成下面的对话，然后和同学一起表演对话的内容。
Complete the following dialogues, and act them out with your classmates.

（1）A：_____要下雨了。

　　B：可不是。你还在路上吗？还是_____到公司_____？

　　A：我_____到公司_____。

　　B：要雨伞吗？_____需要_____，我_____给你送。

　　A：不用了，谢谢你！

（2）A：国庆节_____要到了，你打算怎么过？

　　B：我打算_____　_____。

A：签证办_____了吗？

B：签证快_____办好_____。

6 用下面的词语介绍一下儿自己参加某次出境游的经历。
Introduce one of your experiences of travelling to another country or region with the following words.

热情　　好客　　旅途　　出境　　然后　　马上　　要……了

7 听录音，先回答问题，然后和同学一起表演视频的内容。 🔊 18-1
Listen to the recording and answer the questions. Then act out the video with your classmates.

（1）他们谈话的时间大概是哪个月？

（2）女的打算做什么？

（3）女的打算去哪些地方？

8 汉字练习：看汉字笔画笔顺动态图，并跟着书写。
Practice Chinese characters: Look at the animated illustrations of the strokes and the order of strokes of the following characters, and then write them down.

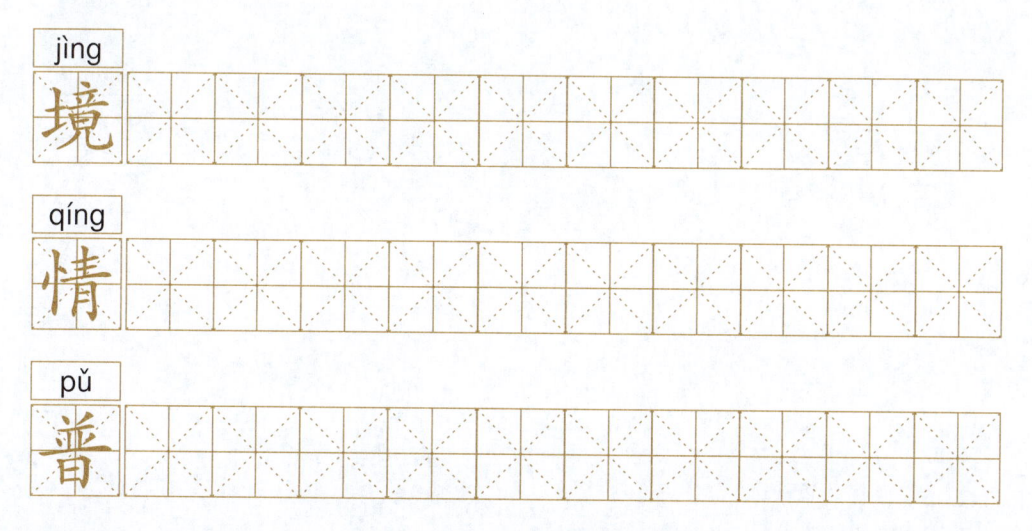

jìng
境

qíng
情

pǔ
普

dǎo
岛

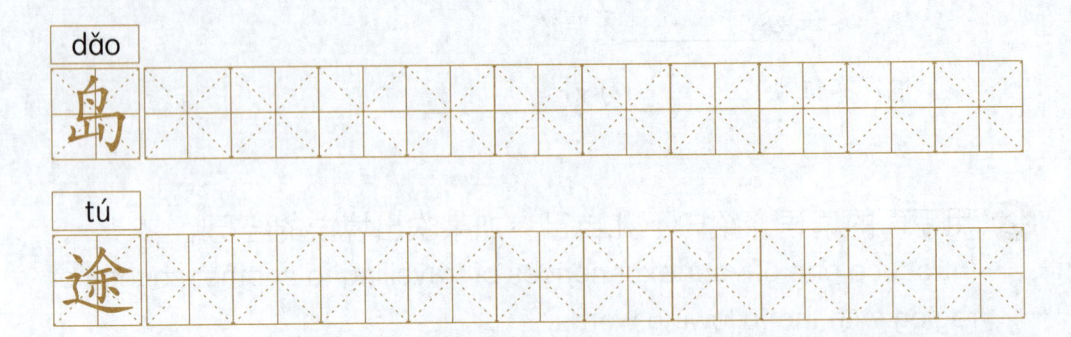

tú
途

第十八课　汉字笔画笔顺动态图

交际项目六
出行交通

第十九课 Lesson 19

Gāosù gōnglù huì bu huì dǔchē ne
高速公路会不会堵车呢

重点提示

- 交际功能：谈论高速公路。
- 主要生词：高速公路、堵车、出行、周边、自驾、容易、办法、提前、主意、错峰。
- 主要语言点：副词"挺"，代词"这"。
- 文化小常识：高速公路。

一 看图讨论 Look at the picture and discuss

1. 下图是什么公路？ What kind of road is in the picture below?
2. 你坐车或开车走过吗？感觉怎么样？ Have you taken or driven a vehicle on this kind of road? How did you feel?

第十九课　高速公路会不会堵车呢

二　课文　Text

听录音回答问题 Listen to the recording and answer the following questions.

1. 他们在谈论什么？ What are they talking about?
2. 李安平打算去哪儿？去做什么？ Where is Li Anping planning to go? What will she do there?
3. 她去的时候要注意什么问题？ What should she pay attention to when she goes there?

Gāosù gōnglù huì bu huì dǔchē ne
高速公路会不会堵车呢 🔊 19-1

Mǎ Wén： Guóqìng Jié nǐ dǎsuàn chūxíng ma?
马　文： 国庆节你打算出行吗？

Lǐ Ānpíng： Wǒ dǎsuàn dào zhōubiān de chéngshì qù wánrwanr.
李安平： 我打算到周边的城市去玩儿玩儿。

Mǎ Wén： Nǐ zuò huǒchē qù háishi zuò qìchē qù ne?
马　文： 你坐火车去还是坐汽车去呢？

Lǐ Ānpíng： Zuò qìchē zǒu gāosù gōnglù tǐng fāngbiàn de.
李安平： 坐汽车走高速公路挺方便的。

Mǎ Wén： Jiàqī gāosù gōnglù huì bu huì dǔchē ne?
马　文： 假期高速公路会不会堵车呢？

Lǐ Ānpíng： Jiàqī zìjià chūxíng de rén duō, shì róngyì dǔchē.
李安平： 假期自驾出行的人多，是容易堵车。

203

Mǎ Wén： Nà yǒu shénme hǎo bànfǎ ma?
马　文： 那有 什么 好 办法 吗？

Lǐ Ānpíng： Wǒ dǎsuàn tíqián yì tiān chūfā.
李安平： 我 打算 提前 一 天 出发。

Mǎ Wén： Zhè shì gè hǎo zhǔyi.
马　文： 这 是 个 好 主意。

Lǐ Ānpíng： Zhè jiào cuòfēng chūxíng.
李安平： 这 叫 错峰 出行。

三 〉生 词　New words　19-2

1. 高速公路		gāosù gōnglù	expressway
高速	形容词	gāosù	high-speed
公路	名词	gōnglù	highway
2. 堵车	动词	dǔchē	have a traffic jam
堵	动词	dǔ	stop up, block
3. 出行	动词	chūxíng	travel
4. 周边	名词	zhōubiān	periphery
5. 挺	副词	tǐng	very
6. 自驾	动词	zìjià	drive oneself
7. 容易	形容词	róngyì	easy
8. 办法	名词	bànfǎ	way, method

9. 提前	动词	tíqián	do (sth.) in advance
10. 主意	名词	zhǔyi	idea
11. 错峰	动词	cuòfēng	stagger one's schedule so as to avoid the rush hour, etc.

四 主要语言点 Main language points

1 坐汽车走高速公路挺方便的。

副词"挺"表示"很"的意思，常用于"挺……的"结构。例如：
The adverb "挺" means "very". It is often used in the structure "挺……的". For example:

（1）今天的天气挺热的。
（2）这里的菜挺好吃的。
（3）坐地铁去机场挺方便的。
（4）马文挺想家的。
（5）李安平挺喜欢旅游的。

▶ 视频：19.1 坐汽车走高速公路挺方便的。

2 这叫错峰出行。

句中的"这"是一个代词，用在句子的开头做主语，复指前文提到的某一内容。本句中的"这"复指前文提到的"提前一天出发"。例如：

205

"这" in this sentence is a pronoun used as the subject at the beginning of the sentence, referring to what was mentioned before. "这" in this sentence refers to "提前一天出发". For example:

（1）A: 我想学太极拳，找不到老师，你有什么办法吗？
　　　B: 你可以上网找一些视频（shìpín），照（zhào）着练习。
　　　A: 这是个好主意。

（2）A: "士"和"土"我经常写错，你有什么办法吗？
　　　B: 你可以把它们的动态图（dòngtàitú）放到自己手机上，每天照着写。
　　　A: 这是个好办法。

（3）A: 我的汉语口音不好，你有什么办法吗？
　　　B: 你可以多用微信的语音和中国朋友聊天儿。
　　　A: 这是个好主意。

（4）A: 最后一个题我不会，你可以替（tì）我做吗？
　　　B: 这不行。

▶ 视频：19.2 这叫错峰出行。

五 文化小常识 General knowledge of culture

高速公路

高速公路就是让汽车高速行驶的公路。高速公路有下面这些特点：（1）只供汽车高速行驶，普通行人或非机动车都不准在高速公路上行走或行驶；(2) 能适应汽车120千米每小时或者更高的行驶速度；(3) 设有多个车道，并且在路中央有分隔带，将往返交通完全隔开；(4) 设有立体交叉口；(5) 全线封闭，只准汽车在规定的一些立体交叉口进出。现在，中国很多城市都有高速公路。

Expressway

An expressway is a kind of highway for vehicles to travel at high speed. It has the following characteristics: (1) It is only for vehicles to drive at high speed, and pedestrians or non-motor vehicles are not allowed to walk or drive on it; (2) It can adapt to the driving speed of 120 kilometres per hour or higher; (3) There are multiple lanes and a dividing strip in the middle of the road to completely separate the round-trip traffic; (4) There are interchanges along the expressway; (5) The whole expressway is closed, and vehicles are only allowed to enter and exit the expressway at designated interchanges. Now there are expressways between many cities in China.

六 练习与实践 Exercises and practice

1 听录音，选择你听到的音，然后朗读下面的拼音。 19-3
Listen to the recording and choose the pronunciation you hear, then read the following Pinyin aloud.

（1）出行 — 举行　　　（2）走遍 — 周边
　　chūxíng　jǔxíng　　　　　zǒubiàn　zhōubiān

（3）好书 — 高速　　　（4）公路 — 红土
　　hǎo shū　gāosù　　　　　gōnglù　hóng tǔ

实用交际汉语 3

　　　　zìjià　　chīxià　　　　　　　túcè　　dǔchē
（5）自驾 — 吃下　　　　（6）图册 — 堵车

　　　　nòngqí　róngyì　　　　　cuòfēng　zuògōng
（7）弄齐 — 容易　　　　（8）错峰 — 做工

2 朗读下面的句子，注意语调、语气和停顿。
Read the following sentences aloud, paying attention to the intonation, tone and pause.

（1）国庆节你打算出行吗？
（2）我打算到周边的城市去玩儿玩儿。
（3）你坐火车去还是坐汽车去呢？
（4）坐汽车走高速公路挺方便的。
（5）假期高速公路会不会堵车呢？
（6）假期自驾出行的人多，是容易堵车。
（7）这是个好主意。
（8）这叫错峰出行。

3 连线组成短语，并读一读。
Match the words to make phrases and read them.

出去	驾车
自己	公路
容易	旅游
高速	出行
错峰	堵车

208

第十九课　高速公路会不会堵车呢

4 替换练习。
Substitution drills.

（1）<u>坐汽车</u>走<u>高速公路</u>挺<u>方便</u>的。

骑车上班	快
我们的校园	漂亮
他的汉语水平	高

（2）<u>高速公路</u>会不会<u>堵车</u>呢？

我们	迟到
银行	下班了
手机	没电了

（3）<u>在车少人少的时候出行</u>
　　叫<u>错峰出行</u>。

自己驾车去旅游	自驾游
在网上进行教学	线上教学
在网上买东西	网购

5 连词成句。
Arrange the words to make sentences.

（1）火车　你　坐　去　汽车　还是　去　坐

　　_____？

（2）有　你　好　吗　什么　办法

　　_____？

（3）中秋节　吗　你　回家　打算

　　_____？

（4）堵车　高速　放假　会不会　的　公路　时候

　　_____？

209

（5）驾车　的　高速　自己　挺　走　方便　公路

_____。

6 完成下面的对话，然后和同学一起表演对话的内容。
Complete the following dialogue, and act it out with your classmates.

A：_____过年了，你回家吗？

B：回家过年。自己驾车走高速公路_____方便_____。

A：过年的时候，高速公路_____堵车呢？

B：是_____堵车，我打算提前出发。

A：这是个好_____！

B：这叫_____出行。

7 用下面的词语介绍一下儿自己坐车或者自驾车走高速公路的经历。
Introduce your own experience of taking a car or driving on the expressway with the following words.

高速　挺　堵车　容易　自驾　叫　错峰

8 看视频，先回答问题，然后和同学一起表演视频的内容。
Watch the video and answer the questions. Then act out the video with your classmates.

（1）视频对话中的"这"指的什么？

（2）为什么说"这"是个好主意？

▶ 视频：19.2 这叫错峰出行。

9 汉字练习：看汉字笔画笔顺动态图，并跟着书写。
Practice Chinese characters: Look at the animated illustrations of the strokes and the order of strokes of the following characters, and then write them down.

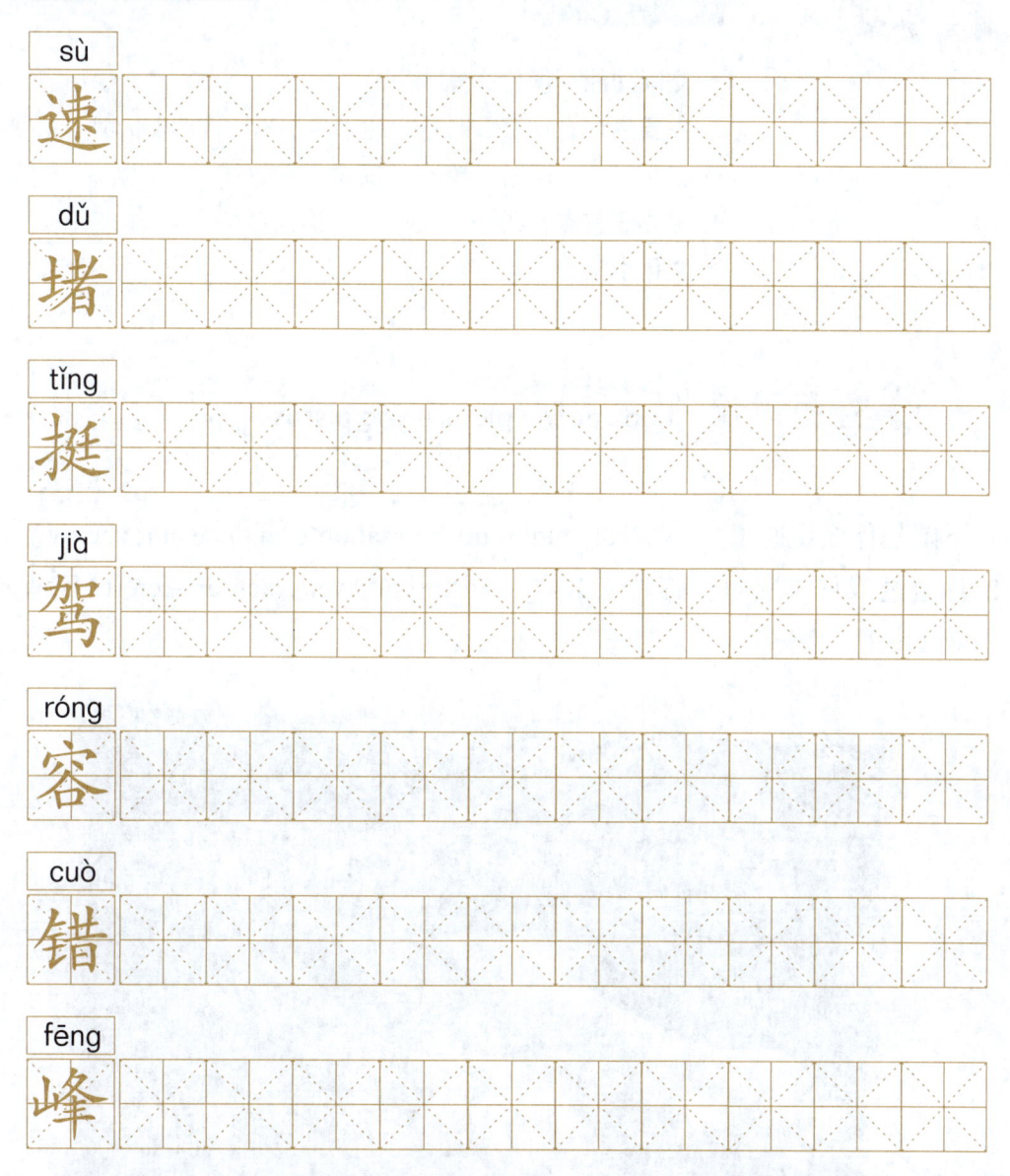

sù
速

dǔ
堵

tǐng
挺

jià
驾

róng
容

cuò
错

fēng
峰

第十九课　汉字笔画笔顺动态图

211

第二十课 Lesson 20

Gāotiě jì kuàisù yòu zhǔnshí
高铁既快速又准时

重点提示

- 交际功能：谈论高铁出行。
- 主要生词：铁路、时速、达到、千米、首选、优势、快速、准时、晚点、安全、舒适。
- 主要语言点：既……又……，连词"甚至"。
- 文化小常识：高铁。

一 看图讨论 Look at the picture and discuss

1. 下图是什么交通工具？ What kind of transportation is in the picture below?
2. 你坐过或见过它吗？感觉怎么样？ Have you ever taken or seen it? How did you feel?

二 课文 Text

听录音回答问题 Listen to the recording and answer the following questions.

1. 他们在谈论什么？ What are they talking about?
2. 马文问了一些什么问题？ What questions did Ma Wen ask?
3. 李安平是怎么回答这些问题的？ How did Li Anping answer these questions?

Gāotiě jì kuàisù yòu zhǔnshí
高铁既快速又准时 🔊 20-1

Mǎ Wén: Shénme shì gāotiě ne?
马 文： 什么 是 高铁 呢？

Lǐ Ānpíng: Gāotiě jiù shì gāosù tiělù, shísù néng dádào liǎng bǎi wǔshí
李安平： 高铁 就 是 高速 铁路，时速 能 达到 两 百 五十

qiānmǐ yǐshàng.
千米 以上。

Mǎ Wén: Zuò gāotiě de rén duō ma?
马 文： 坐 高铁 的 人 多 吗？

Lǐ Ānpíng: Fēicháng duō, xiànzài Zhōngguórén chūxíng yìbān shǒuxuǎn gāotiě.
李安平： 非常 多，现在 中国人 出行 一般 首选 高铁。

Mǎ Wén: Zuò gāotiě chūxíng yǒu nǎxiē yōushì ne?
马 文： 坐高铁 出行 有 哪些 优势 呢？

Lǐ Ānpíng: Gāotiě jì kuàisù yòu zhǔnshí, yìbān bú huì wǎndiǎn.
李安平： 高铁 既 快速 又 准时，一般 不会 晚点。

213

Mǎ Wén: Zuò gāotiě ānquán ma?
马 文：坐高铁安全吗？

Lǐ Ānpíng: Zuò gāotiě hěn ānquán, yě hěn shūshì.
李安平：坐高铁很安全，也很舒适。

Mǎ Wén: Nǎxiē chéngshì yǒu gāotiě ne?
马 文：哪些 城市 有高铁 呢？

Lǐ Ānpíng: Zhōngguó hěn duō chéngshì dōu yǒu gāotiě, shènzhì yìxiē xiǎo
李安平：中国 很多 城市 都有高铁，甚至一些小

chéngshì dōu yǒu.
城市 都有。

三 >> 生 词 New words 🔊 20-2

1. 铁路	名词	tiělù	railway
2. 时速	名词	shísù	speed per hour
3. 达到	动词	dádào	achieve, reach
4. 千米	量词	qiānmǐ	kilometre
5. 首选	动词	shǒuxuǎn	have (sb./sth.) as the first choice
6. 优势	名词	yōushì	advantage
7. 既……又……		jì…yòu…	both...and
既	副词	jì	as well as
又	副词	yòu	and

8. 快速	形容词	kuàisù	fast
9. 准时	形容词	zhǔnshí	on time, punctual
10. 晚点	动词	wǎndiǎn	be behind schedule
11. 安全	形容词	ānquán	safe
12. 舒适	形容词	shūshì	comfortable
13. 甚至	连词	shènzhì	even

四 主要语言点 Main language points

1 高铁既快速，又准时，一般不会晚点。

"既"是一个副词，表示不只某一个方面；"又"也是一个副词，表示几个动作、状态或者情况累加在一起。这两个词合起来构成句式"既……又……"，表示同时具有两个方面的性质或情况。例如：

"既" is an adverb, indicating more than one aspect. "又" is also an adverb, indicating the coexistence of several actions, states or situations. The two characters can be combined to form the pattern "既……又……", indicating having two characteristics or situations at the same time. For example:

> （1）她既会说汉语又会说泰语。
> （2）这里的水果既便宜又好吃。
> （3）王老师的课既好懂又有趣。
> （4）马文的汉字写得既快速又漂亮。

视频：20.1 高铁既快速，又准时。

2 中国很多城市都有高铁，甚至一些小城市都有。

汉语中常用"……，甚至……都……"这一结构表示强调。"甚至"引出要强调的部分，后边用"都、也"与它呼应。这一结构含有比较的语义，表示强调的对象尚且如此，其他的就更不用说了。例如：

In Chinese, the structure "……，甚至……都……" is often used for emphasis. "甚至" introduces the part to be emphasised, and is followed by "都" or "也". This structure shows a comparison, indicating what is emphasised is in such a case, let alone others. For example:

(1) 这个字很难，甚至老师都不认识。
(2) 他有很多字不会写，甚至自己的名字也不会写。
(3) 老师很忙，每天都有课，甚至周末都有课。
(4) 安妮的汉语发音非常标准（biāozhǔn），甚至比一些中国人都标准。

▶ 视频：20.2 甚至一些小城市都有。

五 » 文化小常识 General knowledge of culture

高 铁

高铁就是可以让列车高速行驶的铁路系统。高铁的优点有：(1) 快速，时速在250千米以上。(2) 准时，一般不会晚点。(3) 方便，人们不用提前很长时间去车站等候。现在，中国的很多城市都有高铁。2022年，中国全国高铁运营里程为4.2万千米，排名世界第一。中国的高铁技术很先进，也很安全。迄今为止，中国已经与俄罗斯、泰国、印度尼西亚等多个国家进行了高铁项目的合作。

High-Speed Rail

High-speed rail is a railway system that allows trains to travel at high speed. The advantages of high-speed rail are as follows: (1) It is fast. Trains travelling on it has a speed of more than 250 kilometres per hour; (2) It is punctual. It is usually not behind the schedule; (3) It is convenient. People don't have to arrive well in advance at the station. Nowadays, many cities in China have high-speed rail. By 2022, the operation mileage of high-speed rails in China has reached 42,000 kilometres, ranking first in the world. China has advanced and safe high-speed rail technology and has already cooperated with Russia, Thailand, Indonesia and many other countries on high-speed rail projects.

六 练习与实践 Exercises and practice

1 听录音，选择你听到的音，然后朗读下面的拼音。 20-3
Listen to the recording and choose the pronunciation you hear, then read the following Pinyin aloud.

（1）高铁 gāotiě — 好些 hǎoxiē　　（2）写了 xiěle — 铁路 tiělù

（3）四书 Sì Shū — 时速 shísù　　（4）达到 dádào — 它的 tā de

（5）以上 yǐshàng — 只让 zhǐ ràng　　（6）安检 ānjiǎn — 安全 ānquán

（7）数字 shùzì — 舒适 shūshì　　（8）快速 kuàisù — 坏书 huài shū

实用交际汉语 3
Practical Communicative Chinese

(9) zhǔnshí 准时 — sǔnshī 损失　　　　(10) huán qián 还 钱 — wǎndiǎn 晚点

2 朗读下面的句子，注意语调、语气和停顿。
Read the following sentences aloud, paying attention to the tone, intonation and pause.

(1) 什么是高铁呢？

(2) 高铁就是高速铁路，时速能达到两百五十千米以上。

(3) 坐高铁出行有哪些优势呢？

(4) 高铁既快速又准时，一般不会晚点。

(5) 坐高铁安全吗？

(6) 坐高铁很安全，也很舒适。

(7) 哪些城市有高铁呢？

(8) 中国很多城市都有高铁，甚至一些小城市都有。

3 连词成句。
Arrange the words to make sentences.

(1) 又　高铁　快速　准时　既

_____。

(2) 人　高铁　吗　多　的　坐

_____？

(3) 很　坐　安全　也　高铁　舒适　很

_____。

(4) 哪些　出行　坐　优势　有　呢　高铁

_____？

（5）在 甚至 一些 中国 城市 都 高铁
　　　有 小

_____

_____。

4 替换练习。
Substitution drills.

（1）高铁的时速达到两百五十千米以上。

飞机的时速	八百千米
她的总成绩	三百分
这部手机的价格	一万块

（2）高铁既快速又准时。

她的字写得	快	好
这里的菜	便宜	好吃
在网上学汉语	方便	好懂

（3）中国很多城市都有高铁，甚至一些小城市都有。

他有很多字不会写	自己的名字	不会
网上可以买很多东西	国外的东西	可以买到
她学习非常努力（nǔlì）	吃饭的时候	在看书

219

5 完成下面的对话，然后和同学一起表演对话的内容。
Complete the following dialogue, and act it out with your classmates.

A：现在中国人出行_____坐什么？

B：一般_____高铁。

A：坐高铁有哪些_____呢？

B：坐高铁_____快速_____准时，一般不会_____。

A：坐高铁安全吗？

B：坐高铁很_____，也很_____。

A：是不是只有大城市有高铁呢？

B：很多城市都有高铁，_____一些很小的城市_____有。

6 用下面的词语讨论一下儿自己出行喜欢的交通方式及其原因。
Discuss the travel mode you like and explain the reasons with the following words.

高铁　时速　达到　以上　安全　快速　准时　舒适
首选　优势　既……又……　　甚至……也……

7 看视频，先回答问题，然后和同学一起表演视频的内容。
Watch the video and answer the questions. Then act out the video with your classmates.

（1）女的认为高铁有哪些优势？

（2）坐高铁快不快？晚点的时候多不多？

（3）你坐过高铁吗？感觉是不是像课文中说的那样？

▶ 视频：20.1 高铁既快速，又准时。

8 汉字练习：看汉字笔画笔顺动态图，并跟着书写。
Practice Chinese characters: Look at the animated illustrations of the strokes and the order of strokes of the following characters, and then write them down.

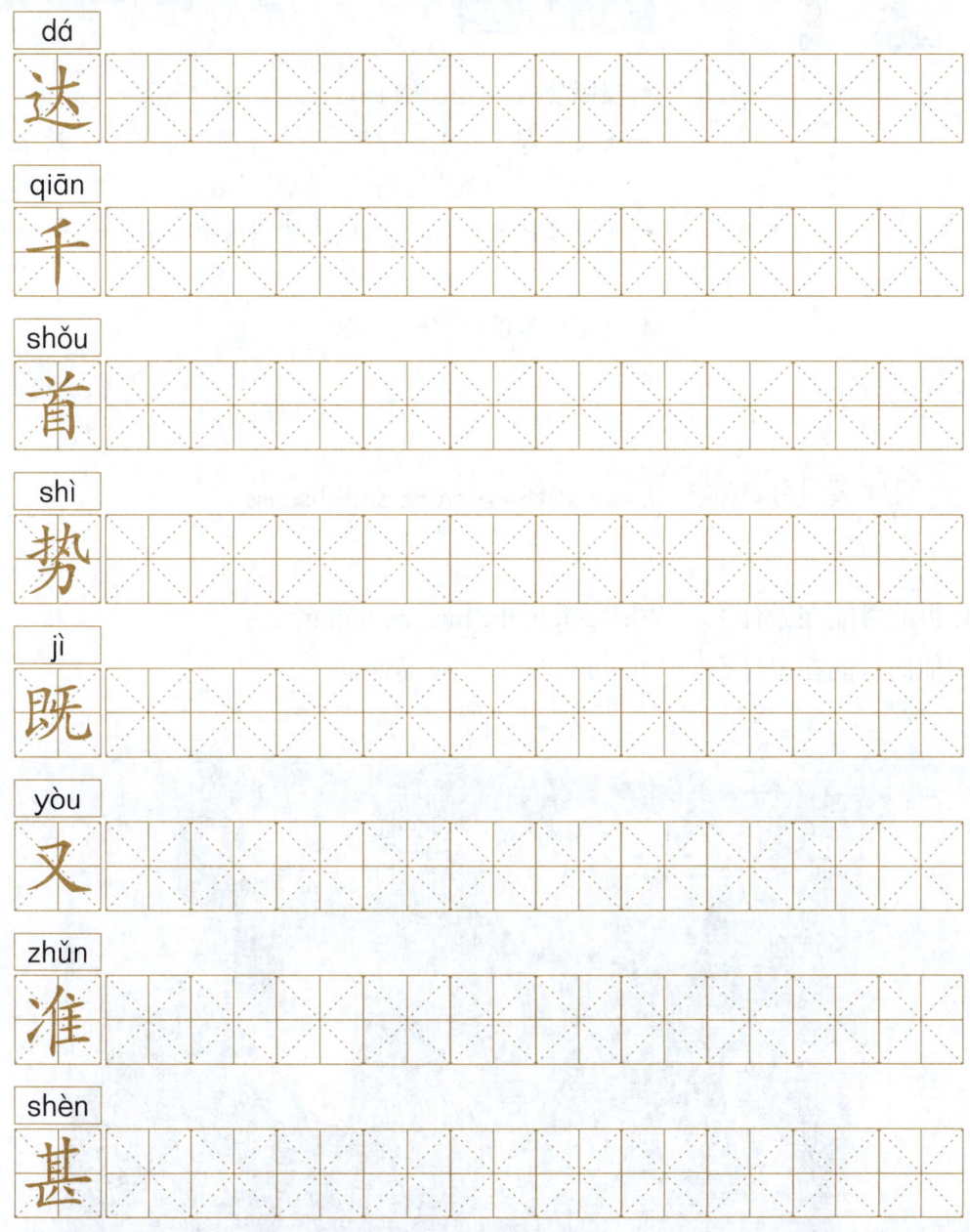

dá
达

qiān
千

shǒu
首

shì
势

jì
既

yòu
又

zhǔn
准

shèn
甚

第二十课　汉字笔画笔顺动态图

第二十一课 Lesson 21

Wǒ de xíngli chāozhòngle méiyǒu
我的行李超重了没有

重点提示

- 交际功能：谈论乘机出行。
- 主要生词：行李、超重、托运、出示、护照、禁止、携带、物品、安检、通道、直行。
- 主要语言点："没有"构成的正反疑问句，句式"……就可以了"。
- 文化小常识：乘机注意事项。

一 看图讨论 Look at the picture and discuss

1. 男的可能在做什么？ What might the man be doing?
2. 他们可能在说什么？ What might they be saying?

222

二 课文 Text

听录音回答问题 Listen to the recording and answer the following questions.

1. 马文可能在哪儿？他想做什么？ Where could Ma Wen be? What did he want to do?
2. 马文问了一些什么问题？ What questions did Ma Wen ask?
3. 女的是怎么回答这些问题的？ How did the woman answer these questions?

Wǒ de xíngli chāozhòngle méiyǒu
我的行李超重了没有 🔊 21-1

Mǎ wén: Nín hǎo! Qǐngwèn zhèr kěyǐ bànlǐ xíngli tuōyùn ma?
马 文： 您好！请问 这儿可以办理行李托运吗？

gōngzuò rényuán: Nín yào qù nǎlǐ ne?
工作 人员： 您要去哪里呢？

Mǎ wén: Qù Tàiguó de Mànɡǔ.
马 文： 去泰国的曼谷。

gōngzuò rényuán: Kěyǐ, qǐng chūshì yíxiàr nín de hùzhào.
工作 人员： 可以，请 出示一下儿您的护照。

Mǎ wén: Hǎo de. Wǒ de xíngli chāozhòngle méiyǒu?
马 文： 好的。我的行李 超重了 没有？

gōngzuò rényuán: Méiyǒu. Xínglixiāng li yǒu jìnzhǐ xiédài de wùpǐn ma?
工作 人员： 没有。行李箱里有禁止携带的物品吗？

Mǎ wén: Méiyǒu.
马 文： 没有。

实用交际汉语 3
Practical Communicative Chinese

gōngzuò rényuán： Zhè shì nín de xínglidān, qǐng náhǎo!
工作 人员： 这是您的行李单，请拿好！

Mǎ wén： Xièxie! Qǐngwèn ānjiǎn tōngdào wǎng nǎr zǒu?
马 文： 谢谢！请问安检通道往哪儿走？

gōngzuò rényuán： Xiān wǎng yòu guǎi, ránhòu zhí xíng liǎngbǎi mǐ jiù
工作 人员： 先往右拐，然后直行两百米就

kěyǐ le.
可以了。

Mǎ wén： Xièxie nín!
马 文： 谢谢您！

gōngzuò rényuán： Bú kèqi!
工作 人员： 不客气！

三 ▶ 生词 New words 🔊 21-2

1. 行李	名词	xíngli	luggage, baggage
2. 超重	动词	chāozhòng	be overweight
3. 托运	动词	tuōyùn	check, consign
4. 出示	动词	chūshì	show
5. 护照	名词	hùzhào	passport
6. 行李箱	名词	xínglixiāng	suitcase
箱	名词	xiāng	box, case
7. 禁止	动词	jìnzhǐ	prohibit

224

8. 携带	动词	xiédài	carry
9. 物品	名词	wùpǐn	article
10. 行李单	名词	xínglǐdān	luggage bill
11. 安检	动词	ānjiǎn	security check
12. 通道	名词	tōngdào	aisle
13. 直行		zhí xíng	go straight

四 主要语言点 Main language points

1 我的行李超重了没有？

这是一句在句尾加"没有"构成的正反疑问句，它的基本形式为"……了+没有"，用于提出某个问题。例如：

This is an affirmative-negative question formed by adding "没有" at the end of the sentence. Its basic structure is "……了 + 没有", which is used to raise a question. For example:

（1）他来了没有？
（2）你们到了没有？
（3）你的感冒好了没有？
（4）茶凉了没有？
（5）大家的作业做完了没有？

▶ 视频：21.1 我的行李超重了没有？

2 先往右拐，然后直行两百米就可以了。

"就可以了"用在陈述句末尾，构成"……就可以了"句式，表达把事情往轻里说的意味。例如：

"就可以了" is used at the end of a declarative sentence to form the pattern "……就可以了", which means "that's all". For example:

（1）A：老师，申请表需要校长签字（qiānzì）吗？
　　　B：不用，你交给我就可以了。
（2）A：老师，学习太极拳难吗？
　　　B：不难，你和大家一起练习就可以了。
（3）A：图书馆离这儿远吗？
　　　B：不远，你往前走一百米就可以了。
（4）A：作业要写在作业本上吗？
　　　B：不用写，口头（kǒutóu）回答（huídá）就可以了。
（5）你不用去她家，给她打个电话就可以了。

▶ 视频：21.2 直行两百米就可以了。

五 文化小常识 General knowledge of culture

乘机注意事项

乘飞机出行的最大优势是快速。人们长途旅行时一般会选择乘坐飞机出行。不过，乘飞机时要注意：（1）需要提前到达机场，以便有足够的时间办理行李托运、过海关安检等各种手续；（2）托运的行李不能超重，否则要另外交费；（3）不能带打火机等各种危险品；（4）有些物品过海关时必须申报。

Precautions for Taking a Flight

The most remarkable advantage of travelling by plane is speediness. People usually choose to take a flight for long-distance travel. However, it is important to note when travelling by plane: (1) It is necessary to arrive at the airport in advance to have enough time for baggage check-in, customs security check, and various other procedures; (2) Checked luggage cannot be overweight, otherwise additional fees will be charged; (3) Lighters and any other dangerous goods are not allowed to be taken along; (4) Some items must be declared to customs.

六 练习与实践 Exercises and practice

1 听录音，选择你听到的音，然后朗读下面的拼音。 🔊 21-3
Listen to the recording and choose the pronunciation you hear, then read the following Pinyin aloud.

（1）请您 — 行李　　　（2）托运 — 多云
　　qǐng nín　xíngli　　　　　tuōyùn　duōyún

（3）超重 — 早上　　　（4）请示 — 禁止
　　chāozhòng　zǎoshang　　　qǐngshì　jìnzhǐ

（5）携带 — 接待　　　（6）吃惊 — 直行
　　xiédài　jiēdài　　　　　chījīng　zhí xíng

　　　　ānquán　　ānjiǎn　　　　　　　tōngdào　tóngdào
（7）安全 — 安检　　　　（8）通道 — 同道

2 朗读下面的句子，注意语调、语气和停顿。
Read the following sentences aloud, paying attention to the intonation, tone and pause.

（1）请问这儿可以办理行李托运吗？

（2）请出示一下儿您的护照。

（3）我的行李超重了没有？

（4）行李箱里有禁止携带的物品吗？

（5）这是您的行李单，请拿好！

（6）请问安检通道往哪儿走？

（7）先往右拐，然后直行两百米就可以了。

3 连线组成短语，并读一读。
Match the words to make phrases and read them.

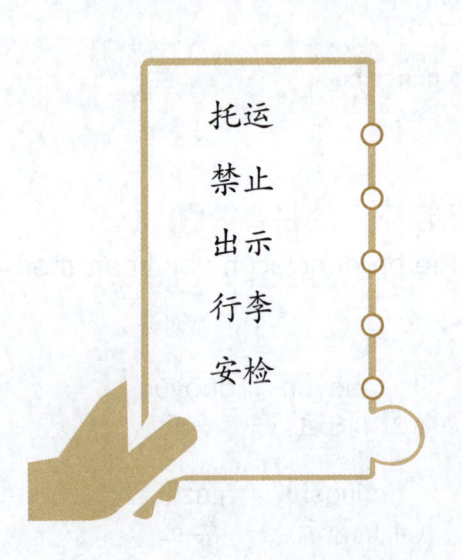

托运　　　　　　通道
禁止　　　　　　护照
出示　　　　　　单
行李　　　　　　行李
安检　　　　　　携带

4 替换练习。
Substitution drills.

(1) 请问这儿可以<u>办理行李托运</u>吗？
- 邮寄（yóujì）药物
- 停车
- 买机票

(2) <u>我的行李</u> <u>超重</u>了没有？
- 你的作业　做完
- 我的邮件　你收到
- 机票　　　买好

(3) 请问<u>安检通道</u>往哪儿走？
- 登机口（dēngjīkǒu）
- 购票窗口（chuāngkǒu）
- 大楼的出口

(4) <u>先往右拐</u>，然后<u>直行两百米</u>就可以了。
- 往前走　　　　往右拐五十米
- 填一下儿表　　交给我
- 过一下儿安检　办理托运

5 完成下面的对话，然后和同学一起表演对话的内容。
Complete the following dialogue, and act it out with your classmates.

A：请问这儿可以＿＿＿＿行李吗？

B：可以。箱子里有＿＿＿＿ ＿＿＿＿的物品吗？

A：没有。我的行李＿＿＿＿了＿＿＿＿？

B：没有，您放上去就可以了。

A：请问海关＿＿＿＿往哪儿走？

B：先＿＿＿＿左拐，然后直行一百米就＿＿＿＿了。

A：谢谢！

❻ 用下面的词语介绍一下儿自己坐飞机的经历，包括托运行李和过安检的过程。

Talk about your experience of taking a flight, including the process of baggage check-in and security check with the following words.

托运　超重　禁止　携带　安检　通道　直行　拐 ……就可以了

❼ 看视频，先回答问题，然后和同学一起表演视频的内容。

Watch the video and answer the questions. Then act out the video with your classmates.

（1）男的问了什么问题？
（2）工作人员是怎么回答他的？
（3）工作人员说"就可以了"是什么意思？

▶ 视频：21.2 直行两百米就可以了。

❽ 汉字练习：看汉字笔画笔顺动态图，并跟着书写。

Practice Chinese characters: Look at the animated illustrations of the strokes and the order of strokes of the following characters, and then write them down.

lǐ
李

chāo
超

第二十一课 我的行李超重了没有

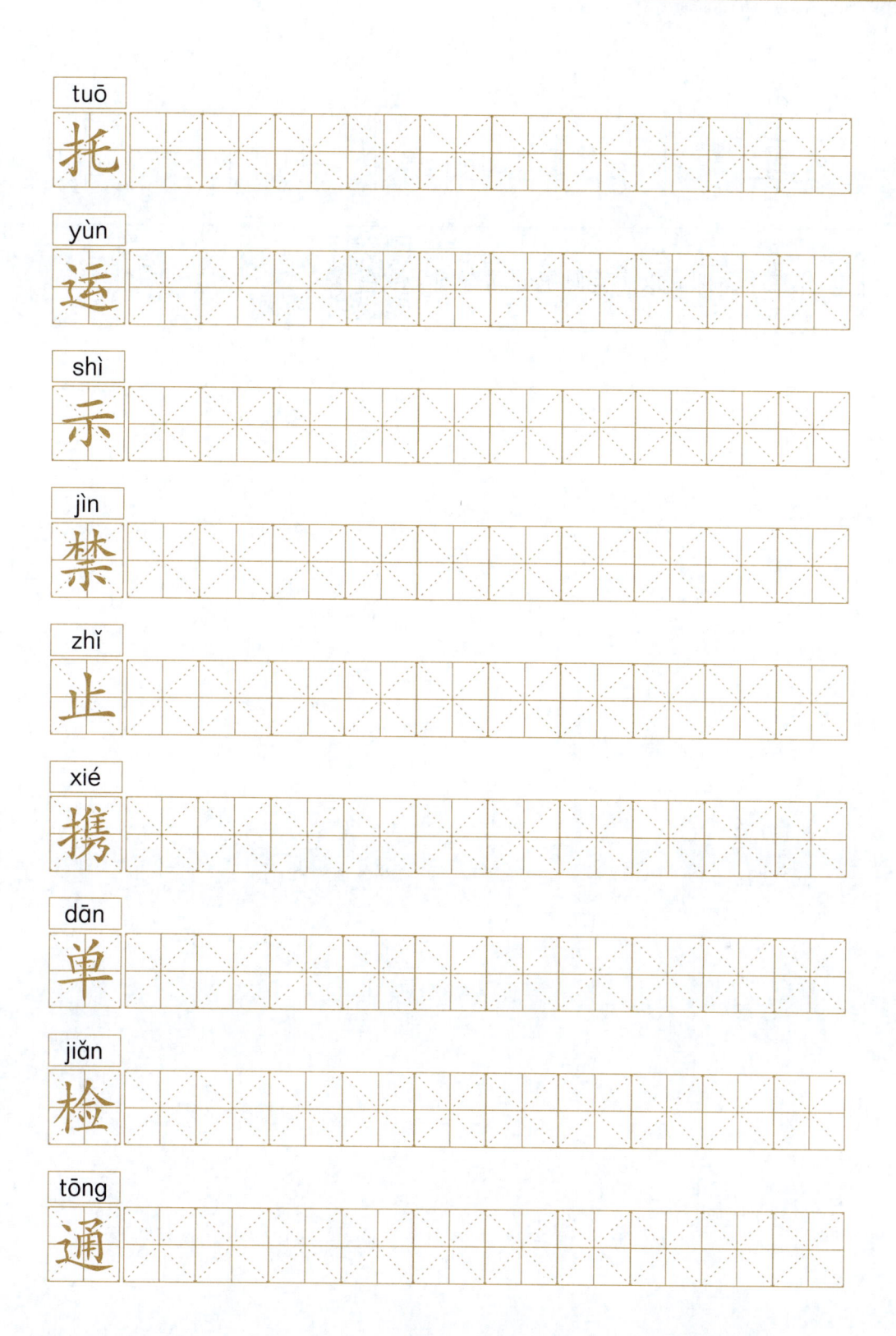

tuō	托
yùn	运
shì	示
jìn	禁
zhǐ	止
xié	携
dān	单
jiǎn	检
tōng	通

zhí
直

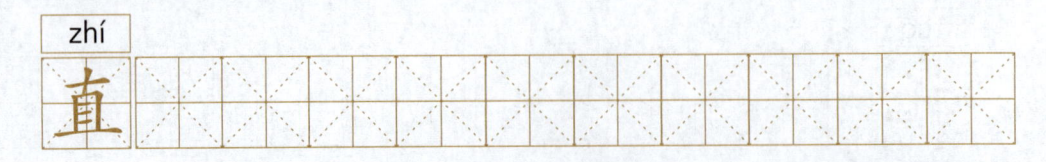

第二十一课　汉字笔画笔顺动态图

综合实践二

第二十二课 Lesson 22

Nín xiǎng dìng shénmeyàng de fángjiān
您想订什么样的房间

重点提示

- 交际功能：办理酒店入住手续。
- 主要生词：双人间、入住、查、空。
- 主要语言点：什么样，有没有，正好。
- 文化小常识：酒店的房间类型。

一 看图讨论 Look at the picture and discuss

1. 男的可能在哪儿？他想做什么？ Where could the man be? What did he want to do?
2. 他们会说些什么呢？ What might they say?

二 课文 Text

听录音回答问题 Listen to the recording and answer the following questions.

1. 马文想做什么？ What did Ma Wen want to do?
2. 女的问了一些什么问题？ What questions did the woman ask?
3. 马文是怎么回答这些问题的？ How did Ma Wen answer these questions?

Nín xiǎng dìng shénmeyàng de fángjiān
您想订什么样的房间 22-1

fúwùyuán: Nín hǎo! Zhèlǐ shì Zhōujì Jiǔdiàn, qǐngwèn nín xūyào bāngmáng ma?
服务员：您好！这里是洲际酒店，请问您需要帮忙吗？

Mǎ Wén: Wǒ xiǎng yùdìng yí ge fángjiān.
马 文：我想预订一个房间。

fúwùyuán: Nín xiǎng dìng shénmeyàng de fángjiān?
服务员：您想订什么样的房间？

Mǎ Wén: Wǒ xiǎng dìng yí ge shuāngrénjiān.
马 文：我想订一个双人间。

fúwùyuán: Nín shénme shíhou rùzhù?
服务员：您什么时候入住？

Mǎ Wén: Shí yuè yī hào rùzhù.
马 文：十月一号入住。

fúwùyuán: Dǎsuàn zhù duōjiǔ ne?
服务员：打算住多久呢？

Mǎ Wén: Shí yuè wǔ hào líkāi, yígòng sì gè wǎnshang.
马 文：十月五号离开，一共四个 晚上。

fúwùyuán: Qǐng shāo děng, wǒ chá yíxiàr nà jǐ tiān yǒu méiyǒu kōng
服务员：请 稍 等，我查一下儿那几天有 没有 空

fángjiān.
房间。

Mǎ Wén: Hǎo de.
马 文：好的。

fúwùyuán: Xiānsheng, zhènghǎo hái yǒu.
服务员：先生， 正好 还 有。

Mǎ Wén: Hǎo de, qǐng bāng wǒ yùdìng yíxiàr, xièxie!
马 文：好的，请帮 我预订 一下儿，谢谢！

fúwùyuán: Bú kèqi!
服务员：不客气！

三 生词 New words 22-2

1. 什么样	代词	shénmeyàng	what kind of
2. 洲际酒店	专有名词	Zhōujì Jiǔdiàn	InterContinental Hotel
3. 双人间	名词	shuāngrénjiān	double room
4. 入住	动词	rùzhù	check in

5. 住	动词	zhù	stay, live
6. 查	动词	chá	check
7. 有没有		yǒu méiyǒu	Is there any...?
8. 空	形容词	kōng	empty
9. 正好	副词	zhènghǎo	as it happens

四 主要语言点 Main language points

1 您想订什么样的房间？

汉语中，可以用"什么样"来询问某人或某事物的特点。"什么样"在句子中做定语，修饰被询问的人或事物。例如：

In Chinese, "什么样" is used to ask about the characteristics of someone or something. It is used as an attribute in a sentence to modify the person or thing being inquired. For example:

（1）你喜欢什么样的衣服？
（2）你打算买什么样的手机？
（3）他的新房是什么样的？
（4）我们的汉语老师是什么样的老师？

▶ 视频：22.1 您想订什么样的房间？

❷ 请稍等，我查一下儿那几天有没有空房间。

这句中的"有没有"不表示疑问，而是表示说话人对某种情况的一种不确定的陈述。例如：

"有没有" in this sentence does not indicate a doubt, but shows the speaker's uncertain statement about a situation. For example:

（1）我也不知道明天有没有课。
（2）稍等，我上网查一下儿有没有这本书。
（3）我看看这家店有没有华为（Huáwéi）手机。
（4）A：你的笔可以借给我用一下儿吗？
　　　B：不好意思，我没有带，你看马文有没有。

▶ 视频：22.2 我查一下儿那几天有没有空房间。

❸ 先生，正好还有。

这句中的"正好"做副词，表示某种巧合（多指时间、情况、适合条件等），意思与"恰好、正巧"差不多。例如：

"正好" in this sentence is used as an adverb, indicating a coincidence (mostly referring to the time, situation, suitable condition, etc.). It is similar to "恰好" or "正巧" in meaning. For example:

（1）我想找他的时候，他正好来电话了。
（2）这件衣服的大小正好适合你。
（3）今天考试的最后一题，昨晚我正好复习到了。
（4）A：你可以借点儿钱给我吗？
　　　B：没问题，我正好取了钱。

▶ 视频：22.2 我查一下儿那几天有没有空房间。

五 文化小常识 General knowledge of culture

酒店的房间类型

根据客人的不同需求和用途，酒店一般会配备不同类型的客房。按照房间的大小和档次分为如下几大类：（1）单人间，房内设一张单人床，供一人住宿。（2）双人间，房内设两张单人床或一张双人床，可供两人住宿。（3）豪华间，房内设的床和双人间一样，只是其他设施的档次高些。（4）套间，一般由两间或两间以上的房间组成，其他设施的档次也很高。此外，还有园景房（面向花园）、湖景房（面向湖水）、海景房（面向大海）等。人们出行时可以根据实际需要选择。

Hotel Room Types

Hotels usually have different types of guest rooms based on different needs and purposes of guests. According to the size and grade of the rooms, they are divided into the following categories: (1) Single room. There is a single bed in the room for one guest. (2) Double room. There are two single beds or one double bed in the room, which can accommodate two guests. (3) Deluxe room. The beds in the room are the same as those in a double room, but it has other better facilities. (4) Suite. It usually consists of two or more rooms with high-quality facilities. In addition, there are also garden-view rooms (facing the garden), lake-view rooms (facing the lake) and sea-view rooms (facing the sea). People can choose suitable types of rooms based on their actual needs when they travel.

实用交际汉语 3
Practical Communicative Chinese

六 》 练习与实践 Exercises and practice

1 听录音，选择你听到的音，然后朗读下面的拼音。 🔊 22-3

Listen to the recording and choose the pronunciation you hear, then read the following Pinyin aloud.

（1）jiù — zhù
　　 就 — 住

（2）dìng — tīng
　　 订 — 听

（3）chá — shā
　　 查 — 沙

（4）qiūtiān — jiǔdiàn
　　 秋天 — 酒店

（5）rùzhù — lùchū
　　 入住 — 露出

（6）líkāi — nǐ cāi
　　 离开 — 你猜

（7）chènzǎo — zhènghǎo
　　 趁早 — 正好

（8）shénmeyàng — zěnmeyàng
　　 什么样 — 怎么样

（9）kōng fángjiān — shuāngrénjiān
　　 空 房间 — 双人间

2 朗读下面的句子，注意语调、语气、重音和停顿。

Read the following sentence aloud, paying attention to the intonation, tone, stress and pause.

（1）您想订什么样的房间？

（2）我想订一个双人间。

（3）您什么时候入住？

（4）打算住多久呢？

（5）我查一下儿那几天有没有空房间。

（6）正好还有空房间。

3 替换练习。
Substitution drills.

（1）您想订什么样的房间？

看	电影
买	笔
听	歌
借	书

（2）我查一下儿有没有空房间。

三人间
华为手机
那本书
这种地方

（3）我们正好还有空房间。

我	也去书店
老师	在办公室
马文	来了电话
现在	没有人坐

4 连词成句。
Arrange the words to make sentences.

（1）了　一课　正好　这　复习　我

_____。

（2）正好　来　电话　他　了

_____。

（3）看看　本　书　网上　有没有　这　我

_____。

（4）有　的　一些　家　酒店　这　房间　什么样

_____？

241

（5）些 水果 超市 家 这 有 什么样 的

_____?

（6）一下儿 老师 课 问 看 明天 有没有 我

_____。

5 完成下面的对话，然后和同学一起表演对话的内容。
Complete the following dialogues, and act them out with your classmates.

（1）A：你想住_____的宿舍？

B：我想住两人一间的宿舍。

（2）A：您想买_____的衣服？

B：我想买一条裙子。

A：我这里_____有两件最新的，您试试。

（3）A：请问您想住_____的房间？

B：有双人间吗？

A：稍等，我查一下儿，_____还有。

B：太好了！

6 用下面的词语讲述一下儿自己预订酒店的经过。
Talk about your experience of booking a hotel room with the following words.

入住　订　离开　单人间　双人间　住　正好　什么样　有没有

7 看视频，先回答问题，然后和同学一起表演视频的内容。
Watch the video and answer the questions. Then act out the video with your classmates.

（1）女的在做什么？

（2）男的想做什么？

（3）男的想要的东西有吗？你是怎么知道的？

▶ 视频：22.2 我查一下儿那几天有没有空房间。

8 汉字练习：看汉字笔画笔顺动态图，并跟着书写。
Practice Chinese characters: Look at the animated illustrations of the strokes and the order of strokes of the following characters, and then write them down.

zhōu
洲

jì
际

diàn
店

shuāng
双

rù
入

chá
查

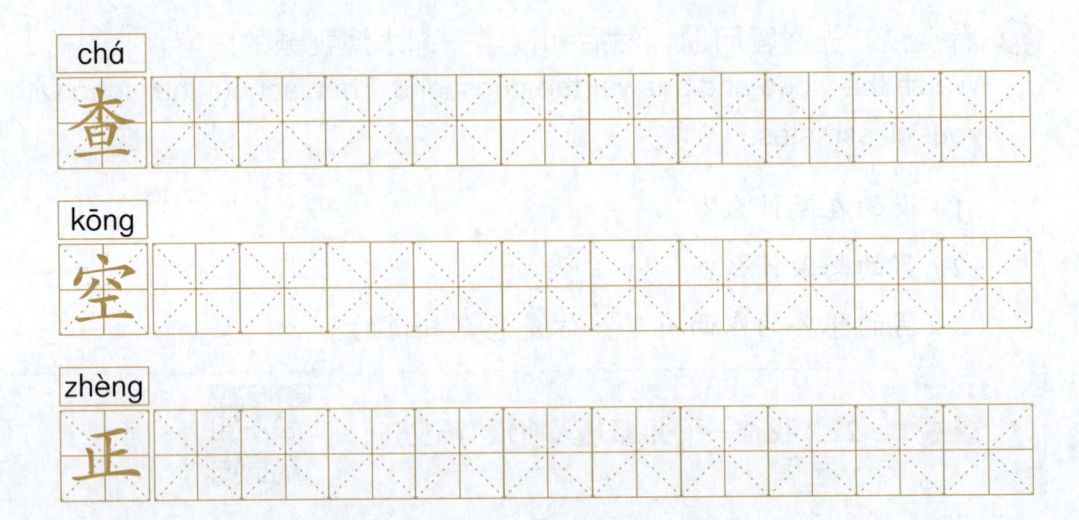

kōng
空

zhèng
正

第二十二课　汉字笔画笔顺动态图

Lesson 23 第二十三课

Qǐngwèn nín yào dǎchē ma
请问您要打车吗

重点提示

- **交际功能**：谈论乘坐出租车。
- **主要生词**：打车、高铁站、后备箱、高峰、时段。
- **主要语言点**：表概数的"左右"，看起来。
- **文化小常识**：网约车

一 看图讨论 Look at the picture and discuss

1. 男的可能想做什么？ What might the man want to do?
2. 男的可能和出租车司机说些什么呢？ What might the man talk about with the taxi driver?

245

实用交际汉语 3
Practical Communicative Chinese

二 课文 Text

听录音回答问题 Listen to the recording and answer the following questions.

1. 马文要去哪里？他准备怎么去？ Where is Ma Wen going? How is he going there?
2. 马文问了出租车司机一些什么问题？ What questions did Ma Wen ask the taxi driver?
3. 出租车司机是怎么回答这些问题的？ How did the taxi driver answer these questions?

Qǐngwèn nín yào dǎchē ma?
请问您要打车吗？ 🔊 23-1

sījī: Nín hǎo! Qǐngwèn nín yào dǎchē ma?
司机： 您好！请问您要打车吗？

Mǎ Wén: Shìde.
马 文： 是的。

sījī: Nín yào qù nǎr?
司机： 您要去哪儿？

Mǎ Wén: Qù gāotiězhàn.
马 文： 去高铁站。

sījī: Hǎo de, xíngli kěyǐ fàng zài hòubèixiāng li.
司机： 好的，行李可以放在后备箱里。

Mǎ Wén: Dào nàr xūyào duō cháng shíjiān?
马 文： 到那儿需要多长时间？

246

司机：Bù dǔchē dehuà, yí ge xiǎoshí zuǒyòu kěyǐ dào.
司机：不堵车的话，一个小时左右可以到。

Mǎ Wén: Kěshì xiànzài lùshang kàn qǐlái hěn dǔ a.
马 文：可是现在路上看起来很堵啊。

司机：Xiànzài shì yǒudiǎnr dǔ.
司机：现在是有点儿堵。

Mǎ Wén: Wèi shénme ne?
马 文：为什么呢？

司机：Yīnwèi xiànzài zhènghǎo shì gāofēng shíduàn. Wǒmen zǒu gāosù
司机：因为现在正好是高峰时段。我们走高速

zěnmeyàng?
怎么样？

Mǎ Wén: Hǎo de.
马 文：好的。

三 生词 New words 23-2

1. 打车	动词	dǎchē	take a taxi
2. 高铁站	名词	gāotiězhàn	high-speed rail station
3. 后备箱	名词	hòubèixiāng	(car) trunk
4. 左右	名词	zuǒyòu	*used after a numeral to indicate approximation*

5. 看起来		kàn qǐlái	seem, appear
6. 高峰	名词	gāofēng	peak
7. 时段	名词	shíduàn	period of time

四 主要语言点 Main language points

1 不堵车的话，一个小时左右可以到。

汉语中，"左右"可以用在数量词后面表示概数，如"三点左右、五个左右、十年左右"。例如：

In Chinese, "左右" can be used after a quantifier to indicate an approximate number, such as "三点左右", "五个左右", and "十年左右". For example:

（1）他三十岁左右。

（2）今天的最高温度在 35℃ 左右。

（3）我今天八点左右到学校。

（4）A：马文有多高？

　　B：他一米八左右。

（5）A：她学了多长时间的汉语？

　　B：她学了一年左右的汉语。

▶ 视频：23.1 一个小时左右可以到。

2 现在路上看起来很堵啊。

汉语中,"看起来"的意思是,通过"看"对某一方面进行估计、评价。例如:

In Chinese, "看起来" means to estimate or evaluate some aspect after "looking" at it. For example:

(1) 今天看起来要下雨。
(2) 看起来你这次考得很好。
(3) 他看起来像外国人。
(4) A: 飞机怎么还没有来?
 B: 看起来是晚点了。
(5) A: 他们两个是兄弟吗?
 B: 看起来不像(xiàng)是兄弟。

视频:23.1 一个小时左右可以到。

五 文化小常识 General knowledge of culture

网约车

网约车是网络预约出租汽车的简称,属于出租车的一种,但是和普通出租车在服务方式、车辆标准和价格等方面有较大差别。在中国,下载相关的约车软件,或者打开微信、百度地图等应用程序,人们都可以预约打车。打开这些软件或程序后,选择网约车或者普通出租车,输入出发地和目的地就可以完成预约。2022年,中国网约车用户达到4.37亿人。

249

Online Ride Hailing in China

Online ride hailing, a type of taxi, is the Chinese abbreviation for online taxi booking. However, in contrast to regular taxis, it is quite different in terms of service method, vehicle standard, and price. In China, people can book a ride by downloading ride hailing software or using Apps such as WeChat and Baidu Maps. Open the software or App, select online ride hailing or taxi, and enter the places of departure and destination. Then, the booking is done. In 2022, the number of Chinese online ride hailing users has reached 437 million.

六 练习与实践 Exercises and practice

1 听录音，选择你听到的音，然后朗读下面的拼音。 🔊 23-3
Listen to the recording and choose the pronunciation you hear, then read the following Pinyin aloud.

(1) yā ā
呀 — 啊

(2) zǒu tóu
走 — 头

(3) fēng dēng
登 — 峰

(4) dǎchē dà chē
打车 — 大车

(5) suǒyǒu zuǒyòu
所有 — 左右

(6) kǎofēn gāofēng
考分 — 高峰

(7) shíduàn zhǐ suàn
时段 — 只算

(8) hòubèixiāng liúshuǐzhàng
后备箱 — 流水账

(9) gǎn jǐ tái kàn qǐlái
赶几台 — 看起来

2 朗读下面的句子，注意语调、语气、重音和停顿。
Read the following sentences aloud, paying attention to the intonation, tone, stress and pause.

（1）请问您要打车吗？

（2）您要去哪儿？

（3）行李可以放在后备箱里。

（4）到那儿需要多长时间？

（5）不堵车的话，一个小时左右可以到。

（6）现在是有点儿堵。

（7）我们走高速怎么样？

3 替换练习。
Substitution drills.

（1）<u>现在路上</u>看起来<u>很堵</u>。

这个蛋糕	很好吃
那天妈妈	很生气
昨天爸爸	很累
今天天气	不太好

（2）<u>飞机</u><u>十点左右</u><u>到达</u>。

我们明天八点	出发
他每天六点	起床
这些作业半个小时	可以完成
那辆车十万块	可以买到

（3）<u>想考满分的话</u>，<u>现在就开始复习吧</u>。

你喜欢	就买吧
不下雨	我们一起散步吧
妈妈知道	她一定很生气
明天天气好	我会去找你

251

❹ 连词成句。
Arrange the words to make sentences.

（1）堵车　左右　不　的话　到　能　半个　小时
_____。

（2）正好　高峰　现在　是　时段
_____。

（3）堵　很　看起来　路上　现在
_____。

（4）左右　可以　车站　到　走路　十　分钟　的话
_____。

（5）班　个　每　有　左右　人　三十
_____。

（6）手机　比较　这种　看起来　好
_____。

❺ 完成下面的对话，然后和同学一起表演对话的内容。
Complete the following dialogues, and act them out with your classmates.

（1）A：请问需要_____吗？

　　B：是，请问去飞机场要_____时间？

　　A：不堵车_____，大概半个小时_____可以到。

（2）A：现在路上_____有点儿堵车啊。

　　B：是，现在_____是下班的_____。

　　A：那我们怎么_____呢？

B：我们＿＿＿＿＿＿＿高速公路。

（3）A：那是什么车？＿＿＿＿＿＿＿很快。

B：是，那是高铁，速度每小时250千米＿＿＿＿＿＿＿。

A：那我们坐高铁去北京要＿＿＿＿＿＿＿时间呢？

B：坐高铁去北京要六个小时＿＿＿＿＿＿＿。

6 看视频，先回答问题，然后和同学一起表演视频的内容。
Watch the video and answer the questions. Then act out the video with your classmates.

（1）根据视频，到那里需要多长时间？

（2）谈话时的交通（jiāotōng）情况怎么样？

▶ 视频：23.2 我们走高速怎么样？

7 用下面的词语说说你自己的一次打车经历。
Talk about your experience of taking a taxi with the following words.

打车　左右　看起来　时段　堵　走　的话

8 汉字练习：看汉字笔画笔顺动态图，并跟着书写。
Practice Chinese characters: Look at the animated illustrations of the strokes and the order of strokes of the following characters, and then write them down.

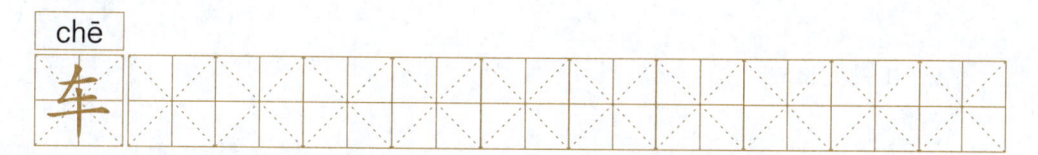

chē
车

实用交际汉语 3
Practical Communicative Chinese

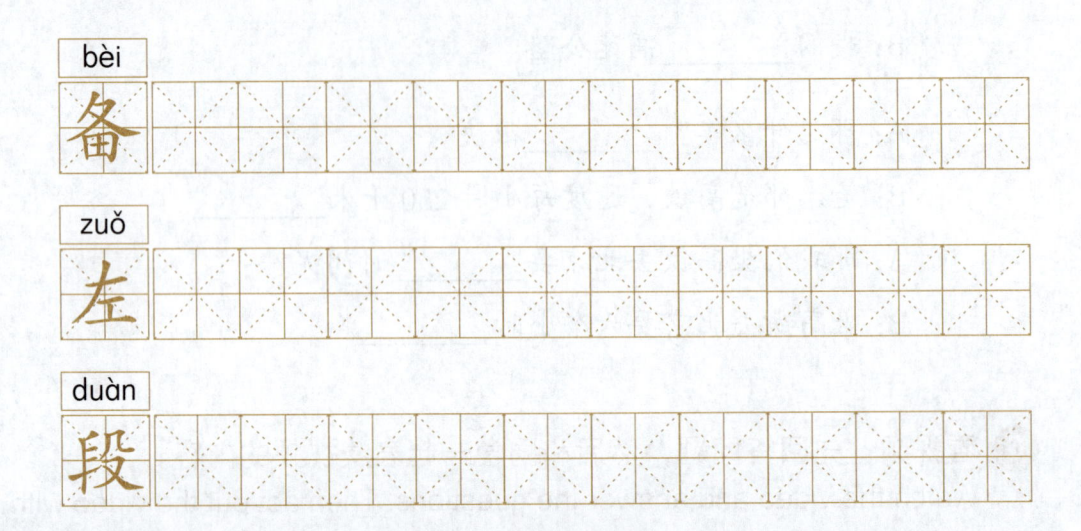

bèi
备

zuǒ
左

duàn
段

第二十三课　汉字笔画笔顺动态图

第二十四课 Lesson 24

Wǒ xiǎng gǎiqiān yíxiàr jīpiào, kěyǐ ma
我想改签一下儿机票，可以吗

重点提示

- 交际功能：改签机票。
- 主要生词：改签、机票、报、次、航班、改、成、已经、满、帮助。
- 主要语言点：介词"从"，是的，已经。
- 文化小常识：改签。

一 看图讨论 Look at the picture and discuss

1. 他买好了机票，但是飞机起飞了，他没有赶上，该怎么办呢？ He bought the air ticket, but the plane has taken off. He missed the plane. What should he do?

2. 他到了机场会和工作人员说些什么呢？ What would he say to the staff after he arrives at the airport?

实用交际汉语 3
Practical Communicative Chinese

二 课文 Text

听录音回答问题 Listen to the recording and answer the following questions.

1. 马文想做什么？ What did Ma Wen want to do?
2. 马文问了工作人员一些什么问题？ What questions did Ma Wen ask the staff?
3. 工作人员是怎么回答这些问题的？ How did the staff answer these questions?

Wǒ xiǎng gǎiqiān yíxiàr jīpiào, kěyǐ ma
我想改签一下儿机票，可以吗 🔊 24-1

Mǎ Wén: Nín hǎo, wǒ xiǎng gǎiqiān yíxiàr jīpiào, kěyǐ ma?
马　文：您好，我想改签一下儿机票，可以吗？

gōngzuò rényuán: Hǎo de, qǐng bào yíxiàr nín de hùzhàohào.
工作人员：好的，请报一下儿您的护照号。

Mǎ Wén: TF-1395569.
马　文：TF-1395569。

gōngzuò rényuán: 9 yuè 15 rì, cóng Guǎngzhōu chūfā de CZ69 cì
工作人员：9月15日，从广州出发的CZ69次

hángbān, shì ma?
航班，是吗？

Mǎ Wén: Shìde.
马　文：是的。

gōngzuò rényuán: Nín xiǎng zěnme gǎi ne?
工作人员：您想怎么改呢？

256

第二十四课 ● 我想改签一下儿机票，可以吗

Mǎ Wén: Gǎichéng 9 yuè 16 rì de CZ90 cì hángbān, kěyǐ ma?
马 文：改成 9月16日的CZ90次航班，可以吗？

gōngzuò rényuán: Qǐng shāo děng! Duìbuqǐ, 9 yuè 16 rì de hángbān yǐjīng
工 作 人 员：请 稍 等！对不起，9月16日的 航班 已经

dìngmǎn le. 17 hào de kěyǐ ma?
订满 了。17号 的 可以吗？

Mǎ Wén: Bùxíng, 17 hào wǒ yǒu shì.
马 文：不行，17号我 有 事。

gōngzuò rényuán: 18 hào hái yǒu kòngwèi, zěnmeyàng?
工 作 人 员：18号还 有 空位，怎么样？

Mǎ Wén: Nà jiù gǎichéng 18 hào ba. Xièxie nín de bāngzhù!
马 文：那就 改成 18号吧。谢谢 您的 帮助！

gōngzuò rényuán: Bú kèqi!
工 作 人 员：不客气！

三 生词 New words 24-2

1. 改签	动词	gǎiqiān	reschedule a ticket
2. 机票	名词	jīpiào	air ticket
3. 报	动词	bào	tell, report
4. 从	介词	cóng	from
5. 次	名词	cì	order, sequence
6. 航班	名词	hángbān	(scheduled) flight

257

7. 改	动词	gǎi	change
8. 成	动词	chéng	become
9. 已经	副词	yǐjīng	already
10. 满	形容词	mǎn	full
11. 帮助	动词	bāngzhù	help

四 主要语言点 Main language points

1 9月15日，从广州出发的 CZ69 次航班，是吗？

汉语中，介词"从"可以和处所词、时间词、方位词一起放在动词前边做状语，表示动作的地点、起始时间、方向等。比如：

In Chinese, the preposition "从" preceding a verb can be used as an adverbial together with a place word, time word or locative word to indicate the place, starting time, or direction of an action. For example:

（1）A：明天我们从哪儿出发？
　　　B：明天我们从学校东门出发。
（2）A：明天的考试要多久？
　　　B：从八点到十点，一共两个小时。
（3）A：为什么很多人喜欢东方？
　　　B：因为太阳是从东方升（shēng）起的。
（4）A：从学校去机场怎么坐地铁？
　　　B：从学校出发，坐三号线可以直达（zhídá）。

视频：24.1 从广州出发的 CZ69 次航班，是吗？

❷ 是的。

汉语中，"是的"表示对别人提出的是非疑问做出肯定回答。例如：
In Chinese, "是的" can be used to make a positive answer to the yes-no question raised by others. For example:

（1）A：他是你的汉语老师吗？
　　　B：是的。
（2）A：这是你的手机吗？
　　　B：是的。
（3）A：你们今天有课，是吗？
　　　B：是的。
（4）A：马文学过汉语，是吗？
　　　B：是的。

▶ 视频：24.1 从广州出发的CZ69次航班，是吗？

❸ 9月16日的航班已经订满了。

"已经"是一个副词，表示动作完成或达到某种程度。例如：
"已经" is an adverb which indicates having completed an action or having reached a certain degree. For example:

（1）菜已经做好了。
（2）A：你的作业做完了吗？
　　　B：我的作业已经做完了。
（3）A：他们出发了吗？
　　　B：他们已经出发了。

（4）A：这节课上完了没有？
　　　B：这节课已经上完了。

▶ 视频：24.2 9月16日的航班已经订满了。

五 文化小常识 General knowledge of culture

改签

旅客买好飞机票或者火车票后，由于航班或列车晚点、取消，以及个人行程更改等，不能按购买的票面上的日期、班次（车次）出发时，可以在飞机或者列车出发前办理更改出发时间和班次（车次）的手续，这就叫改签。办理改签手续一定要在原定出发时间前办理，不同的出行方式和订票方式，所要求的提前的时间也不同。特价票一般不允许改签。

Rescheduling a Ticket

After a passenger has bought a plane/train ticket, if he/she cannot set off on schedule due to flight or train delays, cancellations, or the passenger's personal itinerary changes, he/she can change the departure time and take another flight/train before the plane or train sets off. It is called rescheduling a ticket. The procedures must be completed before the original departure time. Due to different travel modes and booking methods, the time for going through the required procedures also varies. If it is bought at a special offer, it is usually not allowed to be rescheduled.

六 》 练习与实践 Exercises and practice

1 听录音，选择你听到的音，然后朗读下面的拼音。 🔊 24-3
Listen to the recording and choose the pronunciation you hear, then read the following Pinyin aloud.

（1）cì — zhī 次 — 支
（2）shěng — chéng 省 — 成
（3）mǎn — nán 满 — 男
（4）gǎiqiān — kāixiàn 改签 — 开线
（5）xìqiǎo — jīpiào 细巧 — 机票
（6）hángbān — gāng bān 航班 — 刚搬
（7）chídào — zhīdào 迟到 — 知道
（8）yǐjīng — jǐ jīn 已经 — 几斤
（9）chǐzi — zhīchí 尺子 — 支持

2 朗读下面的句子，注意语调、语气和重音。
Read the following sentences aloud, paying attention to the intonation, tone and stress.

（1）9月15日，从广州出发的CZ69次航班，是吗？
（2）您想怎么改呢？
（3）改成9月16日的CZ90次航班，可以吗？

（4）对不起，9月16日的航班已经订满了。

（5）18号还有空位，怎么样？

（6）那就改成18号吧。

3 替换练习。
Substitution drills.

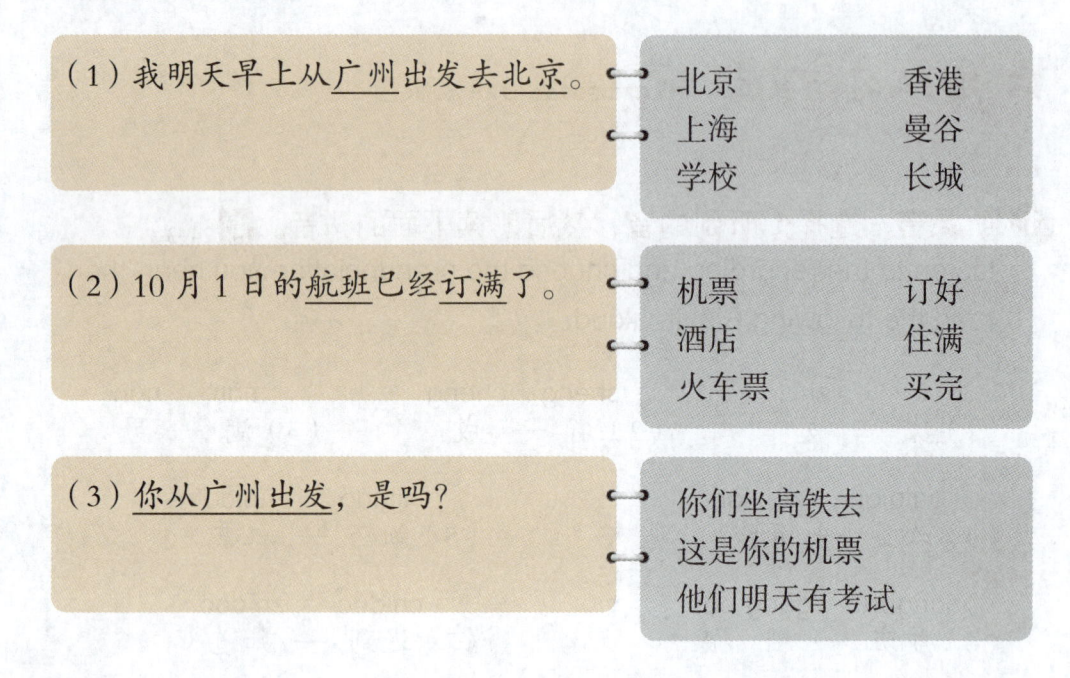

（1）我明天早上从广州出发去北京。

北京	香港
上海	曼谷
学校	长城

（2）10月1日的航班已经订满了。

机票	订好
酒店	住满
火车票	买完

（3）你从广州出发，是吗？

你们坐高铁去
这是你的机票
他们明天有考试

4 连词成句。
Arrange the words to make sentences.

（1）改签　想　机票　我　一下儿

_____。

（2）成　的　改　哪　您　想　航班　天

_____？

（3）满　航班　订　已经　了　这个

_____。

（4）出发　北京　去　从　航班　曼谷　的　是吗

_____？

（5）改　21号　那　航班　成　吧　就　的

_____。

5 完成下面的对话，然后和同学一起表演对话的内容。
Complete the following dialogue, and act it out with your classmates.

小　　　张：您好，我想＿＿＿＿一下儿机票，可以吗？

工作人员：好的。请＿＿＿＿一下儿＿＿＿＿号。

小　　　张：10月1日，＿＿＿＿北京出发的CA1349＿＿＿＿航班。

工作人员：您想改＿＿＿＿哪天呢？

小　　　张：改＿＿＿＿10月4日的CA1619＿＿＿＿航班，可以吗？

工作人员：对不起，这个航班＿＿＿＿预订＿＿＿＿了。

小　　　张：那就改＿＿＿＿10月7日的CA1619＿＿＿＿航班。

工作人员：这个航班可以。

6 用下面的词语说一下儿自己改签机票或者车票的经历。
Talk about your experience of rescheduling a flight or train ticket with the following words.

改签　机票　车票　航班　次　已经　满　成　从　到
已经……了　是的

实用交际汉语 3
Practical Communicative Chinese

7 看视频，先回答问题，然后和同学一起表演视频的内容。
Watch the video and answer the questions. Then act out the video with your classmates.

（1）男的想做什么？
（2）男的要从哪儿出发？
（3）工作人员报的航班号对吗？

▶ 视频：24.1 从广州出发的 CZ69 次航班，是吗？

8 汉字练习：看汉字笔画笔顺动态图，并跟着书写。
Practice Chinese characters: Look at the animated illustrations of the strokes and the order of strokes of the following characters, and then write them down.

gǎi
改

cì
次

háng
航

chéng
成

yǐ
已

264

măn
满

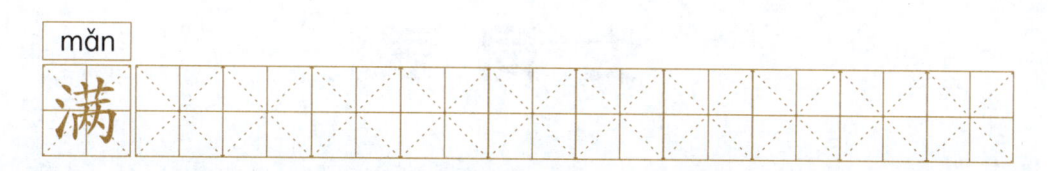

第二十四课　汉字笔画笔顺动态图

生词表

A

安检	动词	ānjiǎn	security check	21
安妮	专有名词	Ānnī	Anne, name of a person	2
安全	形容词	ānquán	safe	20

B

白天	名词	báitiān	daytime	13
白云山	专有名词	Báiyún Shān	Baiyun Mountain	16
办法	名词	bànfǎ	way, method	19
办理	动词	bànlǐ	handle, go through	8
帮忙	动词	bāngmáng	help	7
帮助	动词	bāngzhù	help	24
报	动词	bào	sign up	7
报	动词	bào	tell, report	24
报名表	名词	bàomíngbiǎo	registration form	7
本	代词	běn	this	3
本	量词	běn	a measure word for books	8
毕业	动词	bìyè	graduate	11
表	名词	biǎo	form, table	7
步行	动词	bùxíng	walk	16
部分	名词	bùfen	part	5

C

材料	名词	cáiliào	material	10
操心	动词	cāoxīn	worry about	17

茶叶	名词	cháyè	tea	6
查	动词	chá	check	22
长信公司	专有名词	Chángxìn Gōngsī	Changxin Company	3
超重	动词	chāozhòng	be overweight	21
成	动词	chéng	become	24
吃饭	动词	chīfàn	dining	17
出发	动词	chūfā	set out/off	16
出境	动词	chūjìng	leave a certain district, county, province. etc.	18
出境游	名词	chūjìngyóu	outbound tourism	18
出去	动词	chūqù	go out	16
出示	动词	chūshì	show	21
出行	动词	chūxíng	travel	19
除了……之外		chúle……zhīwài	besides	10
次	名词	cì	order, sequence	24
从	介词	cóng	from	24
从事	动词	cóngshì	be engaged in	1
错峰	动词	cuòfēng	stagger one's schedule so as to avoid the rush hour, etc.	19

D

达到	动词	dádào	achieve, reach	20
打车	动词	dǎchē	take a taxi	23
大会	名词	dàhuì	conference	3
大使馆	名词	dàshǐguǎn	embassy	10

267

	大学	名词	dàxué	university	4
	待	动词	dāi	wait	16
	待会儿		dāihuìr	after a while, later	16
	带	动词	dài	take	6
	但是	连词	dànshì	but	8
	当	动词	dāng	work as	11
	到	动词	dào	to	13
	的话	助词	dehuà	an auxiliary word used after a hypothetical clause	17
	低	形容词	dī	low	14
	地点	名词	dìdiǎn	place	12
	地方	名词	dìfang	place	15
	电脑	名词	diànnǎo	computer	1
	东南风	名词	dōngnánfēng	southeaster	13
	冬天	名词	dōngtiān	winter	15
	堵	动词	dǔ	stop up, block	19
	堵车	动词	dǔchē	have a traffic jam	19
	度	量词	dù	a measure word for temperature	14
	多久	代词	duōjiǔ	how long	8
	多云	名词	duōyún	cloudiness	13
F	发展	名词	fāzhǎn	development	9
	饭	名词	fàn	meal	17
	方法	名词	fāngfǎ	method	5
	方面	名词	fāngmiàn	aspect	1

分明	形容词	fēnmíng	clear, obvious	15
风	名词	fēng	wind	13

G

改	动词	gǎi	change	24
改签	动词	gǎiqiān	reschedule a ticket	24
感谢	动词	gǎnxiè	thank	3
刚才	名词	gāngcái	just now	5
岗位	名词	gǎngwèi	post, job	9
高	形容词	gāo	high	14
高峰	名词	gāofēng	peak	23
高速	形容词	gāosù	high-speed	19
高速公路		gāosù gōnglù	expressway	19
高铁站	名词	gāotiězhàn	high-speed rail station	23
高兴	形容词	gāoxìng	happy	1
各	代词	gè	all, every	5
各种	代词	gèzhǒng	all kinds of	5
跟团游	名词	gēntuányóu	group tour	17
更	副词	gèng	more	6
工作	名词	gōngzuò	work, job	2
公立	形容词	gōnglì	public	4
公路	名词	gōnglù	highway	19
公司	名词	gōngsī	company	3
刮	动词	guā	blow	14
刮风		guā fēng	blow a gust of wind	14
关系	名词	guānxì	relationship	5

	观念	名词	guānniàn	concept, idea	5
	广交会	专有名词	Guǎngjiāohuì	Canton Fair (China Import and Export Fair)	12
	贵	形容词	guì	*(honorific)* your	9
H	还	副词	hái	also	10
	还是	连词	háishi	or	4
	海外	名词	hǎiwài	overseas	4
	汉语	专有名词	Hànyǔ	Chinese language	1
	汉语培训中心	专有名词	Hànyǔ Péixùn Zhōngxīn	Chinese Language Training Centre	7
	航班	名词	hángbān	(scheduled) flight	24
	好处	名词	hǎochù	benefit	6
	好客	形容词	hàokè	hospitable	18
	合作	动词	hézuò	cooperate	12
	后备箱	名词	hòubèixiāng	(car) trunk	23
	护照	名词	hùzhào	passport	21
J	机票	名词	jīpiào	air ticket	24
	吉隆坡	专有名词	Jílóngpō	Kuala Lumpur	2
	级	名词	jí	force	13
	疾病	名词	jíbìng	disease	6
	既	副词	jì	as well as	20
	既……又……		jì…yòu…	both...and	20
	暨南大学	专有名词	Jìnán Dàxué	Ji'nan University	4

嘉宾	名词	jiābīn	honoured guest	3
健康	形容词	jiànkāng	healthy	6
奖学金	名词	jiǎngxuéjīn	scholarship	10
交	动词	jiāo	submit	10
交流	动词	jiāoliú	communicate	12
交往	动词	jiāowǎng	associate, contact	11
郊游	动词	jiāoyóu	picnic	16
教师	名词	jiàoshī	teacher	1
教授	名词	jiàoshòu	professor	3
教学	动词	jiàoxué	teach	4
借	动词	jiè	borrow	8
禁止	动词	jìnzhǐ	prohibit	21
经理	名词	jīnglǐ	manager	3
景点	名词	jǐngdiǎn	scenic spot	18
景区	名词	jǐngqū	scenic area	16
久	形容词	jiǔ	long, for a long time	8
就	副词	jiù	just	6
举办	动词	jǔbàn	conduct, hold	12
觉得	动词	juéde	feel, think	9

K

开心	形容词	kāixīn	glad	1
看病	动词	kànbìng	see a doctor	5
看起来		kàn qǐlái	seem, appear	23
空	形容词	kōng	empty	22
快速	形容词	kuàisù	fast	20

L

来自	动词	láizì	come from	1
老	形容词	lǎo	of long standing, old	3
老人	名词	lǎorén	the aged	17
雷阵雨	名词	léizhènyǔ	thundershower	13
冷	形容词	lěng	cold	14
离开	动词	líkāi	leave	9
礼物	名词	lǐwù	gift, present	6
理论	名词	lǐlùn	theory	5
联系	动词	liánxì	contact	1
零	数词	líng	zero	14
零下		líng xià	below zero	14
留学	动词	liúxué	study abroad	4
留学生	名词	liúxuéshēng	overseas student	4
龙井	名词	lóngjǐng	Longjing, a famous Chinese tea	6
旅途	名词	lǚtú	journey	18

M

马来西亚	专有名词	Mǎláixīyà	Malaysia	2
马力	专有名词	Mǎ Lì	Ma Li, name of a person	3
马上	副词	mǎshàng	immediately	18
满	形容词	mǎn	full	24
曼谷	专有名词	Màngǔ	Bangkok	1
慢性病	名词	mànxìngbìng	chronic disease	5
贸易	名词	màoyì	trade	12
美	形容词	měi	beautiful	16
面试	动词	miànshì	interview	9

名	量词	míng	*a measure word for people*	1
名片	名词	míngpiàn	*business card*	1

N

哪里	代词	nǎlǐ	*where*	15
哪些	代词	nǎxiē	*which, what*	5
南方	名词	nánfāng	*south*	15
女士	名词	nǚshì	*Ms., madam*	3

P

培训	动词	péixùn	*train*	7
培训班	名词	péixùnbān	*training course*	7
朋友	名词	péngyou	*friend*	2
偏	形容词	piān	*inclined to one side*	14
偏北风	名词	piānběifēng	*northerly wind*	14
普吉岛	专有名词	Pǔjí Dǎo	*Phuket*	18

Q

气候	名词	qìhòu	*climate*	15
气温	名词	qìwēn	*air temperature*	14
千米	量词	qiānmǐ	*kilometre*	20
签证	名词	qiānzhèng	*visa*	11
签证官	名词	qiānzhèngguān	*visa officer*	11
晴天	名词	qíngtiān	*fine day*	13
全球	名词	quánqiú	*the whole world*	9
全球性	名词	quánqiúxìng	*global*	9
缺点	名词	quēdiǎn	*disadvantage*	17

273

R

让	动词	ràng	let	6
热	形容词	rè	hot	15
热情	形容词	rèqíng	enthusiastic, warm-hearted	18
人体	名词	réntǐ	human body	5
荣幸	形容词	róngxìng	honoured (to do sth.)	2
容易	形容词	róngyì	easy	19
如果	连词	rúguǒ	if	17
入住	动词	rùzhù	check in	22

S

商贸	名词	shāngmào	commerce and trade	2
上山	动词	shàngshān	climb a mountain	16
上旬	名词	shàngxún	the first ten-day period of a month	12
摄氏度	量词	shèshìdù	centigrade	14
申请	动词	shēnqǐng	apply	9
申请表	名词	shēnqǐngbiǎo	application form	10
身体	名词	shēntǐ	physical constitution, health	6
什么样	代词	shénmeyàng	what kind of	22
甚至	连词	shènzhì	even	20
时段	名词	shíduàn	period of time	23
时间	名词	shíjiān	time	8
时速	名词	shísù	speed per hour	20
世界	名词	shìjiè	world	6
适合	动词	shìhé	fit, suit	5
手续	名词	shǒuxù	procedure	8

	首选	动词	shǒuxuǎn	have (sb./sth.) as the first choice	20
	舒适	形容词	shūshì	comfortable	20
	双人间	名词	shuāngrénjiān	double room	22
	私立	形容词	sīlì	private	4
	四季	名词	sìjì	four seasons	15
	所	量词	suǒ	a measure word for universities, schools, hospitals, etc.	4
T	它	代词	tā	it	11
	特别	副词	tèbié	especially	5
	提交	动词	tíjiāo	submit	10
	提前	动词	tíqián	do (sth.) in advance	19
	天气	名词	tiānqì	weather	13
	填	动词	tián	fill	7
	铁观音	名词	tiěguānyīn	Tieguanyin, a famous Chinese tea	6
	铁路	名词	tiělù	railway	20
	挺	副词	tǐng	very	19
	通道	名词	tōngdào	aisle	21
	托运	动词	tuōyùn	check, consign	21
W	完	动词	wán	finish	16
	晚点	动词	wǎndiǎn	be behind schedule	20
	晚间班	名词	wǎnjiānbān	night class	7
	万	数词	wàn	ten thousand	4

	王文	专有名词	Wáng Wén	Wang Wen, name of a person	3
	为什么		wèi shénme	why	9
	五一	专有名词	Wǔ-Yī	May 1st, International Labour Day	18
	物品	名词	wùpǐn	article	21
X	下	动词	xià	(of rain, snow, etc.) fall	14
	下雪		xià xuě	snowfall	14
	夏天	名词	xiàtiān	summer	15
	先生	名词	xiānsheng	Mr., sir	3
	箱	名词	xiāng	box, case	21
	携带	动词	xiédài	carry	21
	行李	名词	xíngli	luggage, baggage	21
	行李单	名词	xínglidān	luggage bill	21
	行李箱	名词	xínglixiāng	suitcase	21
	需要	动词	xūyào	need	7
	续借	动词	xùjiè	renew the loan of a library book	8
	选择	动词	xuǎnzé	choose	17
	学历	名词	xuélì	education background	10
	学院	名词	xuéyuàn	school (of a university), college	4
	雪	名词	xuě	snow	14
	旬	名词	xún	period of ten days	12

Y

邀请	动词	yāoqǐng	invite	3
要	助动词	yào	be going to, be about to	18
医学	名词	yīxué	medicine, medical science	5
一会儿	数量词	yíhuìr	a moment	16
疑难杂症		yínán zázhèng	miscellaneous cases of illness that are hard to diagnose and cure	5
已经	副词	yǐjīng	already	24
以后	名词	yǐhòu	later time	2
以前	名词	yǐqián	former time	9
以上	名词	yǐshàng	being over/above a certain point (in position/order/quantity)	15
一般	形容词	yìbān	general	10
一般来说		yìbān lái shuō	in general	17
因为	连词	yīnwèi	because	9
优点	名词	yōudiǎn	merit, virtue	17
优势	名词	yōushì	advantage	20
游玩	动词	yóuwán	go sightseeing, visit	17
有点儿	副词	yǒudiǎnr	a bit	14
有没有		yǒu méiyǒu	Is there any...?	22
有名	形容词	yǒumíng	famous	6
又	副词	yòu	and	20
与	连词	yǔ	and	12
预防	动词	yùfáng	prevent	6
越来越		yuè lái yuè	more and more	11

277

	允许	动词	yǔnxǔ	allow	3

Z

再好不过		zài hǎo búguò	be perfect	6
在校		zài xiào	in school	4
早	形容词	zǎo	early	6
早餐	名词	zǎocān	breakfast	16
招收	动词	zhāoshōu	enroll, recruit	4
整体	名词	zhěngtǐ	entirety	5
正好	副词	zhènghǎo	as it happens	22
证书	名词	zhèngshū	certificate	10
政府	名词	zhèngfǔ	government	10
支持	动词	zhīchí	support	10
直行		zhí xíng	go straight	21
只	副词	zhǐ	only	12
指	动词	zhǐ	indicate	5
至	动词	zhì	to	10
制作	动词	zhìzuò	make	6
治疗	动词	zhìliáo	cure, treat (a disease)	5
中国政府奖学金	专有名词	Zhōngguó Zhèngfǔ Jiǎngxuéjīn	Chinese government scholarship	10
中心	名词	zhōngxīn	centre	7
中雪	名词	zhōngxuě	moderate snow	14
中旬	名词	zhōngxún	the middle ten-day period of a month	12
种	量词	zhǒng	kind, type	5
重视	动词	zhòngshì	attach importance to	5

周边	名词	zhōubiān	periphery	19
周末班	名词	zhōumòbān	weekend class	7
洲际酒店	专有名词	Zhōujì Jiǔdiàn	InterContinental Hotel	22
主持人	名词	zhǔchírén	host/hostess	3
主任	名词	zhǔrèn	director	3
主意	名词	zhǔyi	idea	19
住	动词	zhù	stay, live	22
住宿	动词	zhùsù	stay, put up	17
驻	动词	zhù	be stationed	10
专业	名词	zhuānyè	major	9
准时	形容词	zhǔnshí	on time, punctual	20
咨询	动词	zīxún	consult	12
资助	动词	zīzhù	subsidise	11
自驾	动词	zìjià	drive oneself	19
自由	形容词	zìyóu	free	17
最	副词	zuì	to the highest/lowest degree	5
最好	副词	zuìhǎo	had better	17
左右	名词	zuǒyòu	*used after a numeral to indicate approximation*	23

致　谢

衷心感谢以下各方在教材编写及出版过程中提供的各种帮助！

周小兵教授	北京语言大学教师教育学院
彭小川教授	暨南大学华文学院
赵春利教授	暨南大学中文系
方清明教授	华南师范大学国际文化学院
吴福焕副教授	新加坡南洋理工大学
刘瑜副教授	美国杨百翰大学
付彦白副主任	北京语言大学出版社国际中文教育事业部
武传霞编辑	北京语言大学出版社国际中文教育事业部
张建编辑	北京语言大学出版社国际中文教育事业部
黄瓒辉副教授	中山大学中文系
姜有顺副教授	西南大学国际文化学院
张鹏副教授	云南师范大学华文学院
梁珊珊副教授	华南理工大学国际文化学院
张念副教授	中山大学中文系
张绮助理教授	爱尔兰都柏林城市大学应用语言及跨文化研究学院
王红博士	暨南大学华文学院
常芳清老师	暨南大学华文学院
吴晓明老师	暨南大学华文学院
刘丽宁老师	暨南大学华文学院

教材的编写过程还得到了暨南大学和暨南大学华文学院众多领导和同事的大力支持，在此一并深表谢忱！

暨南大学　王功平
2023 年 5 月